Church Wealth, Ministry Health

Five Pillars of Ministry Growth and Financial Wellness

Sherry Peel Jackson, MACS

Heartworks Publications, LLC
PO Box 1085
Cumming, Georgia 30028
www.heartworkspublications.com

Layout by Ginger Marks
www.DocUmeantDesigns.com

Printed in the United States of America

Library of Congress Cataloging-in-Publication Data

JACKSON, SHERRY PEEL

Church Wealth, Ministry Health
Five Pillars of Ministry Growth and Financial Wellness
ISBN: 978-1-943254-07-1
Church & Clergy Finances
1. Church & Clergy Tax Strategies
2. Church & Clergy Wealth Strategies
3. Church & Clergy Legal Issues

Contents

PILLAR FOUR: PREVENTING MINISTERIAL AND PASTORAL PROSECUTION

PILLAR FIVE: PREPARING FOR PERPETUITY

Foreword

Sherry Jackson is one of the bravest, principle-based, reliable Christians I know who is advising pastors and ministries today on ministry finances. Her pastor, Woodrow Walker, is one of my best friends. He told me personally that through all of her challenges she remained a faithful daughter of the ministry. He continues to stand behind her to this day.

Church Wealth, Ministry Health is a vital tool for managing your church and ministry finances when you are committed to doing everything biblically and also adhering to the rule of law.

From a biblical perspective, I am pleased that she opens her book with a Scripture on integrity from the book of Psalms: "But as for me, I will walk in my integrity" (Psalm 26:11). Private integrity is one of the most vital character qualities of a Christian. It means that you hold the line even when nobody is looking because you are aware of God's presence and acknowledge the oversight of the Holy Spirit over your life.

From a practical perspective, she does not tell you how to manipulate the system and do what you want regardless of tax laws or insurance policies and procedures. She tells you how the system works and how a person of integrity can function within the system and still fulfill the will of God.

These chapters are personal. You will read about some of Sherry's own experiences in this book. You will also read true stories she has pulled from her years of advising others on the topic of ministry finances.

This book is also readable. I encourage you to read every chapter carefully and then follow her advice. I believe you will see significant results in the health of your ministry.

Bishop Wellington Boone
Chief Prelate, Fellowship of International Churches

Acknowledgments

This, my eighth published work, would not have been possible without God the Father loving me, the Lord Jesus Christ saving me and the Holy Spirit indwelling me. I gave my life and my heart to Jesus Christ as Lord and Savior in 1986 and never looked back. I thank Pastor Woodrow and Elder Francine Walker, my spiritual parents, for being the solid rocks that keep me steadfastly following Jesus despite all of the tribulations that I've endured. I thank my biological parents, William and Gloria Peel, for instilling in me the courage to stay true to my convictions, the creativity to think strategically and write succinctly, and the DNA to continue the legacy of entrepreneurship that has manifested in our family for decades.

I thank everyone that specifically contributed to the creation of this work; specifically, the subject matter experts that shared insightful facts, stories and anecdotes that make this work educational yet entertaining and the pastors that shared insight into which topics are important to achieve kingdom advancement. I thank Philip and Ginger Marks and Byron and Tamara Brown for their editing and proofing skills that catch all of my mistakes, duplications and wrong wording. I thank Dr. Rusty Ricketson and his wife at Heartworks Publications for their help in seamlessly getting my books published and printed. I thank Dr. Spencer Holman for the book cover and graphics, and for being an integral part of my life. I thank Bishop Wellington Boone for being a force of nature and having the confidence in me to push me forward while others hesitated. Finally, I thank my children, friends and other family members for bearing with me when I was distant as I sought the Lord on the creation of this book and its accompanying modules. To all of you I say, blessings and thanks.

A Word from the Author

As a retired CPA and CFE, and a former IRS agent I've seen hundreds of church financial disasters and successes. All of the financial success stories have a few things in common; namely, the successful pastors and churches use sound biblical financial principles to operate their churches and personal lives. Many pastors and churches operate without a plan, with no policies and procedures, no financial protocol, no board of directors, and no continuity and contingency plan. These pastors and churches know that there is a better way, but they don't act to pursue it. For this reason, they are putting themselves and their churches at risk of outside scrutiny.

This book is for pastors and churches that want to operate with a spirit of excellence as it pertains to church and personal finances and church operations. It is full of principles that will help you improve your personal and church financial future, as well as the personal finances of the congregation. How do I know it works? For over 25 years I've been involved to some degree with church and pastoral finances. I have assisted pastors with their personal finances and tax matters, as well as church operational budgets, policies, record keeping and strategic planning. In addition, I audited ministers for 2.5 years of my stint as an IRS agent, and I am very familiar with the harmful strategies used to damage the finances and reputations of churches, pastors, and ministry leaders. I am passionate about uplifting the Body of Christ by ensuring that ministers avoid falling into the traps that are often set to thrust them into the negative spotlight while their persecutors acquire fame and recognition in the process.

Following the principles that I share in this book will take ministries from a place of operating haphazardly or just being mediocre to a place of security and prosperity. As a financial teacher, I feel obligated to share this information with any ministry that wants to thrive instead of just surviving week to week. I believe that it is my calling to help ministries become financially free, stress and worry free, and be in a position to do the work that the Lord called them to do. I feel that it is a privilege for me to share with you the steps that will allow you, your ministry, and your congregation to prosper for generations to come!

Minister Sherry Peel Jackson

PILLAR ONE

PRESERVING FINANCIAL AND ADMINISTRATIVE INTEGRITY

Why is Having Financial and Administrative Integrity Important?

"But as for me, I will walk in my integrity" (Psalm 26:11a).

Integrity. We hear this word so often that it has become common. However, having integrity is, unfortunately, an uncommon trait—even in many churches. The media delights in reporting the sordid details of fallen pastors and wayward churches. These revelations, however, are only the surface of erosion that started long before their stories hit the airwaves.

In most situations in which news of personal or church wrongdoing has become news, there is also an underlying disintegration of the financial and administrative operations of the ministry. Without proper financial and administrative systems in place even if the church stays out of the media spotlight there will arise hidden issues that surface in church splits, financial collapse, strife, and even governmental intervention.

Our great commission is to seek and save the lost. The unsaved want to see Christ lived out in us; they want to see proof. When ministries don't have consistent policies, when they don't have a solid financial system, when they don't have skills and trustworthy staff, the world will not take them seriously. We must strive to look, act, and think with the great commission in mind. We must make Jesus look good. To do that, we must go the extra mile and put the foundation; the groundwork together or the surface will not be firm. Let's build a firm foundation by making sure our financial and administrative systems are above reproach.

In this pillar, I will discuss ways to preserve financial and administrative integrity in churches and ministries so that your church/ministry stays on one accord and operates with divine order.

WHY IS HAVING A BOARD OF DIRECTORS IMPORTANT?

"Where *there is* no counsel, the people fall; But in the multitude of counselors *there is* safety" (Proverbs 11:14).

Accountability is a part of having integrity. Scripture says that our hearts are deceitful and desperately wicked. Because of this fact, we all need people that will help us stay in line with the plan of God. The enemy lives to make us stumble and fall, especially the pastors and heads of ministries. When these people fall they give an excuse for millions of others to say, "See, I told you there was nothing to that Christianity stuff!"

Churches that are part of denominations have structures in place in which they answer to a council, governing board, or other organizational format. So, these churches and ministries have the necessary coverage.

However, these days thousands of ministries start with one senior pastor and founder. When a ministry is forming it is critical to bring together wise counsel. A group of people that have proven themselves wise and successful will help the ministry grow and make wise decisions. A board of directors should be made up of people that will operate in truth and not just be lackeys to the head pastor. The last thing an up and coming ministry needs is a group of "yes-men" doing the bidding of a novice who needs direction.

It is good to have an odd number of board members so that there won't be any tie votes. Also, it's good to keep the number low so that the board will be effective. Five to seven members should be the maximum so that ministry can go forth without too many competing and composing opinions and ideas.

Here are a few qualifications for membership on a board of directors:

- Informed and available to serve and substantially engaged in ministry
- Committed to the mission of the ministry

- Able to strengthen the ministry due to their expertise
- Highly regarded and respected by others

Here are a few of the duties of a board member:

- Monitor and reinforce ministry programs and services
- Provide relevant financial oversight
- Augment the ministries public status
- Set goals, enact policies and strategic planning

Once you get a group of people together that have the ministries best interest at heart the church or ministry will be on solid ground and ready to move forward in the work of the Lord.

WHY IS HAVING POLICIES AND PROCEDURES ESSENTIAL?

"Now I plead with you, brethren, by the name of our Lord Jesus Christ, *that* you all speak the same thing, and *that* there be no divisions among you, but that you be perfectly joined together in the same mind and in the same judgment" (1 Corinthians 1:10).

Rules. When we were children, we hated rules. "Do this," "don't do that." It seemed like everything we wanted to do was against the rules, and we never got a chance to simply explore our boundaries. In churches and ministries there must be rules and boundaries or there will be an out of control mess. Let me tell you a story.

God's Church in Midland, Georgia was growing by leaps and bounds since the young; new Pastor Baker arrived two years ago. The church was only five years old, but the founding pastor had taken ill and ordained Julius Baker as senior pastor. Once Pastor Baker was installed, he immediately started a social media campaign that attracted hundreds of millennials to the church, and they were allowed to become active members upon joining. David Walton was one of those millennials. He was a very handsome outgoing man with lots of financial ambition. David was only a member for six months before he started hanging around the administrative office and before he went to work on the second shift daily. He would help the ladies by doing some of the janitorial work and even painted the walls in the staff bathroom. The ladies loved it and loved having him around. Pastor Baker was a bi-vocational pastor and didn't even know that David was at the church during many afternoons.

One day David started asking questions about whether the church ever rented the gym or the auditorium out. He knew exactly who to ask—Janice Richards, the single mother of two that obviously had eyes for him. Janice was one of the front desk administrative assistants that worked during the school day hours so that she would be home when her children arrived home from school. Usually when David arrived to help out at the church, Janice was there for at least an hour before she had to leave.

Janice told David that the only time she knew of anyone else ever using the gym or auditorium was when Pastor Baker let other pastors hold events if their churches were not large enough. David got closer and closer to Janice. Eventually, David asked Janice to schedule him for the use of the auditorium for a Saturday one month away because he was an ordained minister from his old church and he wanted to give a workshop that would help people save money on insurance. Because David hinted that he would reward Janice, she went ahead and put David's workshop on the calendar. There weren't any other events that Saturday, but Janice didn't clear it with Pastor Baker or his executive assistant. She figured that if nothing else she would open and close the church for the workshop so nobody else had to be bothered with that task.

A month went by without anyone in else in the administrative office knowing about this scheduled event. Janice had marked the calendar "meeting in the auditorium" but everyone was so busy that no one paid attention or asked what type of meeting. In the meantime, David had been approaching several church members letting them know about the workshop. Of course, because they knew it was to take place at the church, they all thought that Pastor Baker had sanctioned it.

On the day of the workshop, Janice arrived at 8:00 A.M. to let David and his two associates in. The men set up coffee, tea, fruit and Danish—a regular continental breakfast. The workshop registration started at 9:00 A.M., and by 9:30 A.M. when it started there were over 200 people in attendance. Some of them were members but some were invited by David's associates, and some read the advertisements that the trio ran on social media and in local newspapers. The attendance was so high because everyone knew about God's Church and thought that if this church was endorsing the workshop it was legitimate.

The workshop lasted from 9:30 A.M. till noon, and participants were given the opportunity to purchase low-cost life insurance policies. Many took advantage of the deal because David and his associates were very persuasive and dynamic speakers. Overall 40% of the participants bought various types of policies. Janice cleaned up as David and his associates talked to participants well past 1:00 P.M. Janice locked the church at 2:00 P.M.

Sunday morning two of the deacons commented to Pastor Baker about how good the workshop was the day before. He was puzzled and asked for details. After the service, he called the administrative staff into his office for a quick meeting to find out what all this was about. Janice admitted to allowing David Walton to present the insurance information and she apologized for not getting with the executive assistant to obtain approval. She assured Pastor Baker that she didn't receive any money from David and that David assured her that he would donate all of the money he saved by not having to rent a hotel for the event. Pastor Baker reprimanded Janice and let the staff know that under no circumstances was any church property to be rented out or otherwise used by others without his permission.

By the next day at 2:00 P.M. the administrative office had received 23 calls from members and eight calls from non-members asking to schedule a time that they could rent the auditorium to present everything from pain cream to male enhancement products! Pastor Baker had a mess on his hands and had to implement damage control immediately.

Upon looking for any written direction Pastor Baker, the staff and the board of directors realized that there were no policies or procedures in place regarding the use of the church property. As a matter of fact, they discovered that there were no policies and procedures in place at all. There were bylaws from when the church first started, but that had nothing to do with how the church operated on a daily basis and what was allowed or not allowed to take place in the church and on church grounds.

Pastor Baker called an emergency meeting of the board, and on the very next Saturday they sat down for seven hours and carved out a set of new church policies.

Having policies and procedures in place is a great way to curtail any strife and misunderstanding about what is or is not allowable in the church or ministry. To be able to tell a member to review a policy that is already in place will reduce doubt that favoritism, nepotism or any other type of politicking is allowable. Policies and procedures can also save your church from letting the enemy creep in and change the culture of your church from what God has ordained for it.

HOW IMPORTANT IS YOUR ACCOUNTING SYSTEM?

"There are four *things which* are little on the earth, But they *are* exceedingly wise: The ants *are* a people not strong, yet they prepare their food in the summer;" (Proverbs 30:24-25).

In any company or organization one of the main components is the accounting system. "Money makes the world go around" is an old adage, but it is true in that we can't do ministry effectively without money. Money is needed for buildings, salaries, transportation, food, and ministry publications. The proper management of that money can't be understated and when a ministry has a haphazard way of accounting for money disaster looms.

Pastor Little was an old-school pastor who wasn't much for using technology. He also relied on his family and old friends to help him keep the church going. Mrs. Little was the sole financial officer for 18 years, and she kept the books by hand. When Mrs. Little decided to retire, Pastor Little ordained Margie White as Minister of Finance because she went to high school with him and was the smartest in their graduating class. Margie had gone to technical school and received an associates degree in bookkeeping/accounting. She knew that the best way to keep books was no longer by hand, but she wanted to keep the books by ledger, and Pastor Little was fine with that—until the mortgage check bounced six months after Margie came on board. Pastor Little asked Margie how the mortgage check could bounce. That's when he realized that Margie didn't know how to properly record income, expenses, or journal entries at all.

As you can see, having a solid accounting system in place is a must. There are several good computerized accounting systems on the market that will keep track of all giving, other income, assets, salaries, and expenses. Many of these programs will keep track of departmental totals and are able to generate statements of assets and revenues and expenses in real time. These computerized accounting programs cost between $200 and $1,000 but buying a program and having a staff that knows how to use it will ensure that your finances are in order, which will put you and your congregation at ease concerning how the money is accounted for.

WHAT ARE INTERNAL CONTROLS?

"Be diligent to know the state of your flocks, and attend to your herds;" (Proverbs 27:23).

In God's Church, there were four (4) employees: the pastor, the secretary, the receptionist, and the bookkeeper. The bookkeeper only worked part-time three evenings a week because the church board didn't want to pay him enough to work full time. The receptionist answered the phones, got the mail, and occasionally made deposits if funds were low and money came in the mail. With such a small staff at a growing church, as funds started to increase the pastor decided to increase his salary instead of bringing the bookkeeper on full-time.

After the end of the church's third year, the bottom fell out. In January of the fourth year, several members approached the pastor and the bookkeeper claiming that their giving statements were understated by hundreds and even thousands of dollars. The bookkeeper checked his records based on giving envelopes and deposits made. He didn't see anything wrong, so he asked these members to bring in spreadsheets of their giving for that year. That's when he and the pastor had a rude awakening. They discovered that many dates on which the congregants with discrepancies said they had given were not recorded. Digging deeper they found that in each of those cases the giver usually issued a postal money order to the church, via the mail. All of the members with discrepancies regularly sent their tithes and offerings through the mail because either they traveled a lot, or they didn't want to carry cash to the church and/or didn't like online giving.

In each case, the majority of the money orders purchased by the congregants were not recorded in the giving records. When the bookkeeper and pastor sat down and traced the flow of funds, they discovered that the receptionist was collecting the mail, depositing the checks and taking the money orders for herself, cashing them at the local post office. They discovered that it was an easy fix to change the money order from "God's Church" to "Gloria Charles" which was the receptionist's name. She would blot out the memo portion of each money order, and it was discovered that she would go to several different post offices to cash the money orders to avoid raising suspicion. Once Gloria discovered that her scheme had been discovered she vanished without a trace. When the pastor and several deacons went to her apartment, they found an eviction sign posted and, based on looking in the windows; the apartment was abandoned. Once word got out that the receptionist was embezzling money a quarter of the church left—blaming the pastor for not having better control of the church staff and finances.

The receptionist should not have access to deposit slips or signature stamps. The person that makes deposits shouldn't have check signing authority. These are simple fixes to financial office catastrophes.

Internal Controls, as defined in accounting and auditing, is a process for assuring achievement of an organization's objectives in operational effectiveness and efficiency, reliable financial reporting, and compliance with laws, regulations and policies.

When churches are starting and growing the pastor has to be very careful about making sure that controls are in place to safeguard the funds and all sensitive information. If this care is not taken the church can be short-lived.

Also, I have noticed that as churches get larger some become laxer in the day-to-day operations, which can allow a thief to slip in and wreak havoc.

Here are a few internal controls that will help the financial office:

- The person/people that count the money should not deposit the money.
- More than one person should be counting the money.
- The counting room should be locked at all times.
- Rotate out counters every three to six months.
- Use count sheets and have the counters sign the sheets.
- The person that makes the deposits should not be a check signer.
- The person that makes the deposit should not keep the deposit slips if the money is not in a secure/sealed bag.
- The person that retrieves the mail should not count the money or have access to deposit slips.

- The people that count should not have access to editing giving statements.
- Reconcile the bank statements every month.
- Shred all financial information that is no longer needed.
- Have more than one check signer; a trusted member should be one.
- Each check over $1,000 should have two check signers.

Here are a few internal controls that will help in the administrative office:

- Keep all confidential records (giving envelopes and statements, counseling records, member contact information, sensitive mail) under lock and key.
- Limit the number of people that have access to church records. For example, the bookkeeper shouldn't have access to the counseling files.
- Shred all old sensitive member information and counseling information when no longer needed.
- Limit access to the pastor's and minister's private mailboxes.
- Keep the church building and all offices locked when not in use.
- Screen and get a background check on all new employees.

- Limit access to the administrative office area, especially while private meetings are taking place.

HOW IMPORTANT IS SELECTING THE RIGHT STAFF?

"Moreover, it is required in stewards that one be found faithful" (I Corinthians 4:2).

A church or ministry represents the Lord Jesus Christ, and as such, the leadership is responsible for not only ensuring that sound doctrine is taught but also that integrity, honesty, and loyalty are required in the staff that is chosen.

A good staff member is one that is first saved, sanctified, and filled with the Holy Spirit. Also, a good staff member is wise, loyal to Christ and the ministry, and discrete—keeping all that goes on in the church from getting out onto the rumor mill.

When a church doesn't have reliable staff members it is primed for failure from many different directions:

- Staff sharing intimate knowledge of the finances or other situations
- Staff stealing funds or church equipment
- Staff selling insider information to members or rival churches
- Staff blackmailing others on staff
- Staff lying to the pastor and other leaders
- Staff not doing their jobs

For older churches, staff members should be loyal members that have proven their level of maturity and wisdom.

Usually, these are older members, but sometimes the younger members have a lot to offer also.

For new churches, it is hard to gauge people for staff positions but some major areas to look at are:

- Are they faithful members of the church?
- Do they tithe and give offerings?
- Do they have good character outside of the church? This trait must be researched. Spend time with them at home and in other settings.
- At start-up churches, it is wise to start new staff hires off with light duties and work them up to the sensitive areas after they have been proven trustworthy. Even if these members are relatives, it wouldn't be good to throw them right into the fire. Some people aren't spiritually mature enough to handle all that goes on in the workings of a church.

When I first gave my life to the Lord in 1986, I was already an accountant. About two months after attending the church one of the leaders found out that I was an accountant and she took me to the business office and introduced me to the finance director as a CPA candidate. He looked at me and smiled. Looking back at her he said, "She ain't' ready." I was insulted, but in retrospect, I understand exactly what he meant. I was a spiritual babe; I may not have been able to understand how churches operate and the things that have to be done.

If the pastor of a church is Holy Spirit led he or she sometimes makes decisions that other staff members don't understand and are sometimes downright angry about.

Evelyn started in the business office at Victory Lane Church in January. She had just graduated from college with her Bachelors in Business Administration in December, and because the church needed help, she was eager to oblige. Evelyn had been a member of the church since her parents moved to the area when she was in high school, so she knew everyone at this church of 400 members.

Three months after working in the business office the excitement turned to skepticism and then to contempt. Evelyn didn't like the way money was handled in the business office. She didn't have a problem with the funds coming in, but she was bewildered by some of the amounts being paid out. Her greatest concern was a monthly check to Mother Agnes Nelson. Evelyn didn't like mother Nelson because she screamed and shouted loud every Sunday and even got louder than Pastor Willis sometimes. Mother Nelson would also get on the early Morning Prayer calls and take up half the time with her prayers, as if she was showing off.

When Evelyn asked the Chief Financial Officer why Mother Nelson was receiving money from the church monthly she didn't get what she thought was a straight answer. Mother Nelson was by no means impoverished, as she drove a luxury car and lived in a high-end gated community, so Evelyn was perplexed by the payments. After the seventh month Evelyn decided to leave her job at the church and leave the church altogether! She felt that money was perpetually being wasted paying Mother Nelson some kind of either blackmail or hush money.

Evelyn not only let her mind wander about what the payments could be for, but she told her best friend Charla, and a rumor started about Mother Nelson having some "dirt" on Pastor Willis. By the time Evelyn left, word was spreading about the payments, so Pastor Willis ended up having to address it one Sunday during service. He preached about how rumors get started when we don't trust the Lord, and then he revealed that the church was debt-free because Mother Nelson had the funds to help them get a special deal to pay off the church through a mortgage program that had a deadline for participation. The church was $24,000 short in qualifying for the program to eliminate the entire mortgage and Mother Nelson stepped in with a loan that saved the church from having to pay an additional $160,000 in mortgage principal and interest. Pastor Willis told the congregation that Mother Nelson wanted to keep it secret, but she agreed that it was time to reveal it now that rumors about the payments were flying all over the place. Pastor Willis even had the paperwork available for any church member that wanted to verify the facts, but no one was interested in reviewing the documents.

After the sermon the church stood up and clapped for Mother Nelson. Charla immediately called Evelyn with the news. She was on her new job and she hated it. Evelyn was shocked to hear the story, and at first she was going to say the mortgage program story was fake propaganda, until Charla told her that Pastor Willis had all of the paperwork at the service for review.

Having faithful mature staff members can make a church run like the Body of Christ is supposed to function.

Having immature people in administrative and financial functions can be a thorn in a pastor's side. Avoid it at all costs.

WHY ARE FUNDS COUNTING PROCEDURES IMPORTANT?

"He who is faithful in *what is* least is faithful also in much; and he who is unjust in *what is* least is unjust also in much" (Luke 16:10).

I have consulted with several pastors and church business staff members that are not aware that just counting the giving is not enough. Pastors, especially in small churches, depend on two or three "trusted" people to be responsible for counting, recording, and depositing funds. However, there is a lot more to be done with each giving cycle if your church is to ensure accuracy and integrity when it comes down to keeping track of the funds collected.

Washington Street AME Church had been around for over 50 years. Pastor Sandra Fields had become the senior pastor and half the church left because they wanted the dashing Elder Jessie Baker to get the position. Pastor Fields, once she established her spiritual authority, felt that she had a small circle of loyal members, and she chose four of the most loyal ones to count the one offering they had every Sunday.

The church didn't have a lot of bills and Pastor Fields was bi-vocational and didn't take a salary from the church. She wasn't sure how much was coming in on a weekly basis but there was always enough for the utilities and the few office supplies that were needed monthly.

Pastor Fields received a large bonus from her job, so she used these earnings to purchase the land next door to the church because she had a heart for the young people, and she wanted to build a community center for youth. After she fully paid for the land next door, she started inviting guest speakers to speak every fourth Sunday; which was deemed Youth Sunday. The funds raised at these services were put aside for building a nice youth center. The community heard about it and some of them even started to attend and give on fourth Sunday.

During one of their fundraising services Pastor Fields invited Bishop Stanley Chandler to speak. She knew that Bishop Chandler would draw a nice sized crowd because he was a powerful motivator. He told Pastor Fields and the ministers that whatever was raised for him for an honorarium would be immediately given back for the youth center. Pastor Fields was excited and looked forward to the service.

After the powerful message from Bishop Chandler it appeared that everyone in the building got up and gave. Pastor Fields was so excited that she went down to the giving table and started counting up some of the funds. She wanted to get an idea of how much they raised for the building. She didn't count everything herself but the part she did count added up to right at $5,000. "That will take care of the architectural drawings and county fees", she thought.

Two of her trustees, Deacon Wells and Deacon Pope took the buckets in the back so that an accurate count could take place. While they were gone, Pastor Fields decided to have some of the youth come up and share, hoping that the good news about a high giving day would soon come from the back. She was a little concerned when she saw Deacon Wells come back into the sanctuary, so she left her seat to ask him what was going on. Deacon Wells said, "Oh, Pope said he would finish up, I wanted to hear the kids." She then remembered that was not the first time both men went to the back, but Deacon Wells didn't stay. She figured that she had only paid attention this time because of the anticipation of a big number coming from the back.

A few minutes later, after three young people shared about the importance of the Lord in their lives, Deacon Pope emerged from the room with a big smile on his face. Pastor Fields then smiled also, as she motioned for him to come to the podium and announce the total amount collected for the building project. She was taken aback a little when her eyes refocused and she saw that Deacon Pope's wife was walking next to him as he approached the pulpit from the count room. "Where did she come from? Why was she back there?" Pastor Fields thought to herself.

Deacon Pope stood there and asked for a drum roll and then said, "Today we raised $3,717 for the building. That's the largest amount that we have raised so far, and we owe it all to Bishop Chandler."

The entire church was up on their feet praising God—all except for Pastor Fields. "Did I count wrong?" she asked herself as she let that figure roll around in her head. She finally realized that she was sure that she indeed had counted at least $5,000, because she stopped at $5,000 and looked over the table, noticing that so much more needed to be counted.

At this point she had a decision to make. "What do I do?" she thought. "I know that at least $1,300 is missing from the amount I counted, let alone the rest of the money that was counted."

Pastor Fields motioned for the crowd to settle down and sit back down. Then she said, "We are all so excited, but we are going to have to count again because I am sure that number is way low. When we were still receiving funds up here I counted a little over $5,000 before I stopped counting, and there was a lot more money on the table and a lot more still coming."

With that, the crowd started to murmur, and Mrs. Pope got up and headed toward the back, even before her husband could get up. Deacons Pope and Wells got up at the same time, Wells looking puzzled and Pope looking panicked. Pastor Fields and Bishop Chandler also got up and headed towards the count room. Pastor Fields motioned to the choir director and he started playing and the choir started singing.

When Pastor Fields and Bishop Chandler arrived at the count room door the Popes' were squirming and Deacon Wells was trying to find his key, for he was the only one of the two deacons with a key. As he got his key ring out he said to Deacon Pope, "Man what happened, you said you had it under control like you always do. Were you counting too fast?"

Deacon Wells finally got the right key. As he pushed the count room door in it would hardly open. He pushed harder and noticed that dollar bills were stopping the door from opening. As they all looked down they noticed that these dollars were bound in rubber bands. Pastor Fields picked up one of the bundles. It was $1,000 worth of $100 bills. The Popes were silent. Then Deacon Pope said, "Wow, I must have dropped all that on the way out of the room. I knew my bag felt too light." Mrs. Pope was looking down, making sure her eyes didn't meet Pastor Fields. However, Pastor Fields did notice that something was hanging onto the side of Mrs. Pope's purse. "What's this?" Pastor Fields exclaimed as she plucked at the "snag" on the purse. The odd snag turned out to be the corner of a ripped $100 bill! Pastor Fields picked up the other two cash bundles that were stuck under the door and noticed that one of them had a ripped $100 bill that matched the piece plucked from the purse. Not another word was said. The Popes walked out the back door of the church and Pastor Fields announced that the corrected total was $6,717. The Popes were never seen at Washington Street AME again.

Many churches have many loyal members that would never take a penny from the church. However, no church should take that chance. Here are a few steps you can take to ensure that your count is accurate and that all of the funds arrive at the bank.

- Have at least five unrelated people on the count team and rotate them in and out regularly.
- Use count sheets and have the counters verify each other's numbers.
- Have the counters sign off on the count sheets.
- Have someone that is not on the count team make the deposit after the envelope is sealed.
- Have a separate person verify the count sheets and record the deposits.

HOW DO YOU ACCOUNT FOR CONTRIBUTIONS?

"He who tills his land will have plenty of bread, but he who follows frivolity will have poverty enough!" (Proverbs 28:19).

People give to churches with differing motivations. Some love the Lord and want His ministry to go forth. Others want to impress the church leadership and still others think that if they give they can get a loan from the church when they come upon hard times. I've seen it all. So, how does the church account for and treat contributions? I believe the following procedures are the best and simplest way to make sure your member contributions are properly treated.

First, always have offering envelopes available for each offering. It's good to have them labeled with the various giving categories like tithes, offerings, building fund, missions, etc.

Next, make sure you give regular training on the proper completion of these envelopes. It may seem like common sense to you, but I have seen so many different issues with the offering envelopes that many funds counters and donation recorders quit due to the complications.

For example, some women use several different last names and they complete the envelopes each week based on the way they feel while they sit in the pew. Jane may have started out being Jane Peggy Doe. When she first got married she started using Jane Peggy Edwards. Then some months later, for some reason she starts using Jane Doe Edwards, then Jane P. Doe. This name changing throws the envelope recorders into a tizzy. At the end of the year Jane blames the church because her giving statement is deficient by over $1,000 but because she used so many different names the funds were recorded under different accounts.

Another issue with the giving is when people give but don't specify the category. Then at the end of the year they are angry because their statement doesn't reflect the $1,000 they gave to the building fund but didn't check off that category. I have even heard of one man that said the counters were supposed to know (I suppose by osmosis) that the $1,000 check was for the building fund just because it was so much higher than his regular giving. The bottom line is the congregation needs regular reminders about the proper way to complete the envelopes.

A good software system to record the giving is a must. I have seen people still recording giving manually, which can be prone to errors and even manipulation. For example, if you don't have honest people recording the giving someone may be jealous of another member and purposely fail to record some of that person's giving. When there are errors in a computerized giving system mistakes and errors are easily detectable.

Also, it's good to keep a copy of the annual contribution statements of each member. This policy really helps when they come back to the office three years later to ask for the statement so that they can complete tax returns or because they are being audited and they don't have the records anymore. Churches are required to keep records for three years, but I recommend keeping the giving statements over $1,000 for at least five years.

Member contributions are and should be kept confidential. Loyal staff members will not go tell their friends that, "Grady Baker drives a Lexus and lives in a $750,000 house but only gives $100 a month." Or, "That new single guy is giving $7,000 per month so he must be doing pretty well." Make sure that the records are kept locked up and that, when the people that record the giving are ready to print out the weekly or monthly statements, they are not left on the copy machine! Train the recording team to retrieve the statements after each printing run so that the wrong eyes won't see the statements.

Now I need to let you know that there are different types of giving. We are all familiar with general giving, which is used to keep the bills paid. However, many church administrators don't know about restricted funds and specially designated funds.

Let's talk about **restricted funds** first. These funds are funds that the giver retains control of and directs where they are used. When a church receives restricted funds, the donor does **not** receive a tax deduction for the funds given because they do not give the church control of the funds.

When a church accepts restricted funds, it accepts the money with the knowledge that the giver is making the gift for a specific project. The church is obligated to use the funds for that specific project or they must return the funds to the giver. If the church uses the restricted funds for any other purpose there could be grave consequences—from having to repay the funds or even prison time for some of the leadership.

For example, if Richey Banks gave God's Church $100,000 to build a youth recreation center on the four acres at the back of the church, the church has to use all of this money to build a youth center. The pastor, board of directors, elders, or other leaders cannot redirect these funds to any other project, even if the church building itself is falling apart. If any of these funds are used for any other purpose the church leadership could face serious consequences for breach of fiduciary duty because they accepted the funds with the understanding that they would be used for the youth recreation center. The church must give Mr. Banks a receipt for the $100,000 and this receipt must state that the donation is not tax deductible.

An unfortunate abuse of restricted funds that I have personally seen occurs when a high-profile guest minister comes to a small church. People from all over town may come to hear the guest minister and at the end of service they are asked to give an honorarium (love offering) to this pastor. The problem is that sometimes the guest pastor is not given the entire amount collected on his or her behalf. This diversion of funds is a clear abuse of restricted funds.

I have watched as thousands of dollars are collected, taken in a back room and then the guest pastor is presented with a $1,000 check! I was once involved in a conference that had a high-profile minister as the keynote speaker. Originally, I was asked by the minister's team to help with the count, but the host church would not allow me to help with the count. Based on what I did see while I was close to the counters, I know that much more money was collected than the minister was ultimately given.

The host church is operating in deception when they say that a special offering is being taken up for a guest speaker and they only give that person a fraction of the funds collected. This behavior not only damages relationships between pastors and churches but also causes mistrust among the host church's members as they discover dishonesty in their leadership.

Now let's talk about **designated funds.** These funds are designated for a specific purpose, but the church takes control of the funds and is not obligated to use the funds for that purpose alone. As discussed above, when people donate to the missions' ministry, for example, the designations are usually on an offering envelope. If the envelope contains a statement of release to the church, then the gift is tax deductible and the church can use the funds for whatever is needed.

Here is an example of the type of statements that churches use to ensure that the gifts can be repurposed and are tax deductible to the giver: *We sincerely appreciate your financial support; however, the Board of Directors reserves the right to redirect all funds as needed.*

So, in the case of the funds designated for missions being used to pay the electric bill, since the church has control of the funds it can pay the electric bill because that use was in the best interest of the church, and the giver gets a tax deduction for his donation.

In conclusion, make sure that any large donation is carefully documented, and that there is an understanding of the type and purpose of the funds before they are accepted. Some members with means may want to control the church through their giving, so due diligence is always in order.

WHAT PROCEDURES SHOULD BE USED FOR HONORARIUMS?

For the Scripture says, "You shall not muzzle an ox while it treads out the grain," and, "The laborer *is* worthy of his wages" (1 Timothy 5:18).

Earlier I talked about giving honorariums to guest ministers but here I will elaborate on the procedures that should be used.

The IRS considers honorariums, or "love offerings" as many churches call them, to be taxable income to the receiver. As an IRS agent, I audited many pastors that were not including these in income, we will discuss that in the Pillar Protecting the Pastor and the Church From the IRS.

When a guest minister is scheduled to come and speak at your church, they should be sent two forms in advance and you should receive these forms back before they speak. The first form is a W-9. This form contains the information needed to prepare a 1099 Miscellaneous Income form to give the speaker. The speakers will need to list their social security numbers or their ministry Federal ID numbers and sign the form. This form should be collected from anyone that is paid over $600 in a year. Always have it completed because even if a minister only receives a $400 honorarium you may have him speak again later in the year and he may receive another $400, which would put him over the threshold of $600.

The other form is one that you will create on church letterhead. This form will explain that the church needs to collect the payee information. This **Speaker Form** will have spaces to record:

1. The speaker's name
2. The address the speaker wants on the check—whether mailed or hand delivered
3. The name the check should be made out to (personal or ministry)

At the bottom of the form there should be information reiterating that the IRS considers honorariums to be taxable if the payment is made out to the speaker, as opposed to her ministry. I have noted that around 85% of the speakers request the check be made to them personally and only 15% of the speakers have the checks written out to the ministry.

Many churches pay honorariums in cash. This practice is dangerous because it leaves the church open to IRS scrutiny. The only time that honorariums should be paid out in cash is when the guest speaker is not a U.S. citizen and does not have a way to cash a check. For example, many African speakers don't have bank accounts in the states and their home banks don't accept checks from U.S. banks, or it's a hassle for them. In these cases, document the amount of cash given and have the speaker sign a statement acknowledging the receipt of the cash. Your church may have to store up some cash before the speaker arrives because the offerings collected for her may be mostly checks and you don't want to get stuck with no cash to give someone that has $1,000 collected in honorariums. At year end the church accountant is supposed to create 1099 Forms for every non-employee that received over $600 during the year. This group would include contractors and speakers. If the speaker is not a U.S. person the accountant does not have to complete the 1099. Also, if the check was made out to the ministry there is no need for a 1099. The only people that should receive 1099's are those that received payments over $600 as sole proprietors. It helps when the accountant has the names, addresses and ID numbers for each person that was paid over $600.

HOW IMPORTANT IS INSURANCE FOR CHURCHES AND PASTORS?

"*There is* desirable treasure, and oil in the dwelling of the wise, but a foolish man squanders it" (Proverbs 21:20).

I can't say enough about insurance for the church. The purpose of insurance is to be a safety net when things go wrong. The devil is busy so all churches need insurance. There are several different types of insurance and I will discuss a few of them that are critical.

Liability Insurance

This insurance covers a lot, including your physical building in case of fire, flood, theft, and even someone getting hurt while on the premises. A church liability policy will be your most costly insurance policy, but you will be glad you obtained it when disaster strikes. I have heard about church fires on the news for years. However, lately I have heard about more and more church robberies, even during the service! Protect your church, members and visitors by making sure you have a church liability policy.

Automobile Insurance

If your church has buses, vans, or other vehicles that are used to transport members and others you need a very good automobile insurance policy because an accident with members or non-members can result in financial strain on the church.

Peace COGIC had a friends and family day on Saturday, July 14th. They wanted to introduce themselves to the neighborhood because they purchased the building eight months prior. They advertised the event well and even walked around the neighborhoods in the area for a month of Saturdays before the event, handing out flyers and praying with residents. The big day came, and the church utilized the three brand new shiny brightly painted vans to pick up anyone that wanted a ride to the church. The curious, the hungry, and the skeptical alike boarded the vans and went to the event, which was held on the lawn in front of the church. It seemed that everyone was having a good time and that the church was finally being accepted into the community. Then it happened. One of the children started screaming. Everyone ran toward the child, but nobody seemed to know why he was screaming. This seven-year-old boy was screaming so loud that the other children were putting their fingers in their ears and running in the other direction. The child's mother tried to calm him as one of the church members, a medical doctor, fell to her knees and grabbed the child up, taking him into the building as the mother followed. Ants! The child had stepped into an ant bed and had been bitten several times around the ankles.

The doctor comforted the mother and the child, put disinfectant and cream on the bites and everyone went on their way. The mother and child continued to fellowship with the others and when the fun was over everyone went home happy.

However, Tuesday morning the church doorbell rang and in walked a man serving a lawsuit against the church. The lawsuit was filed by the mother of the child the bitten up by the ants. She claimed that her child was in such bad shape that he wasn't able to attend summer camp for the rest of the month and that he was so traumatized by the event that he would not come outside and stand in the grass anymore. The woman was suing the church for $100,000 for pain, suffering, medical bills, and counseling for her son!

The church leadership was devastated. They had only purchased the minimum amount of liability insurance required by the mortgage company—$50,000. They decided to purchase the minimum amount required because they were small and wanted to keep expenses low. The fact that their building was in an underprivileged neighborhood and that they would have lots of unsaved people/non-members in the building due to their evangelism initiatives never came into play in any decisions to purchase insurance.

The pastor and the attending doctor wanted to go and talk to the woman and explain that they were sorry and that they would give her a few thousand dollars for her trouble, but one of the church members that was an attorney advised against visiting the women because a visit may be considered harassment or witness tampering. One of the Peace COGIC members that lived down the street from the woman and her son inquired with another neighbor that was friends with the woman. The church member found out that the boy was just fine, and the woman just wanted money. The mother was a single parent, and this would be her way to get some of the things she wanted in life, she said. She thought the church had lots of money because of the brand-new vans.

From her window, the church member took pictures of the boy playing in his yard and down the street with other children. She took pictures for a week, and even had some pictures showing that the boy was getting on the bus to go to summer camp.

Once she delivered the pictures to the pastor, the pastor gave them to the attorney member and the woman settled for $2,000. After this incident the church board voted to get $500,000 in liability insurance and be mindful of the fact that not everyone has the church's best interest at heart.

Key Man Insurance

This insurance protects the church if something happens to any of the key leaders of the church, especially the pastor. These days many churches are independent churches with a dynamic founder that people flock to the church to hear each week. Whether the church is a Mega-Church or not, funds may stop flowing if the pastor gets ill or worse, passes away. Key man insurance will be there to fill the void until decisions are made concerning a new pastor. If people leave when the pastor is no longer in the pulpit the giving goes down drastically. Thus, the key man insurance will help pay the bills and salaries during the gap between pastors. Insurance for the family of the pastor is also in order.

Insurance Riders

If you let other organizations or even individuals rent out space on church property these groups need to purchase insurance riders. The riders should be for at least

$1,000,000 and cover everything a liability insurance policy covers including building damage and accidents. If someone is using your church gym, for example, and a child falls and breaks his leg, the renting group's rider insurance should cover that injury and the church's insurance should not be involved in the matter.

Worker's Compensation

Again, assuming that everyone, even employees, doesn't have the church's best interest at heart, it is best to have good worker's compensation insurance. Some employees work hard and may get hurt while doing their job. Some employees may simply want to "get over" and they may create an injury to get time off work or even to have the church pay them long-term for an injury not caused at the church.

Joe was a maintenance man at Brown Memorial Baptist Church. Joe hated his job and resented the fact that most of the office staff had flexible hours while he had to be at work from 8:30 am to 5:00 pm. Because Joe only had a high school diploma his salary was low, and he was making half of what some of the office staff workers made. Over time Joe became bitter. He got a night job that paid by the hour. One night Joe hurt his ankle on this night job while mopping the floor. He knew that he had no recourse on this independent contractor night job, but he knew that the church had insurance. The next morning, he arrived at work early, and concealed his injury from the one person that beat him to work. Within minutes of arriving there was a loud crash and the one staff member went running down the hall to see what happened. There was Joe, on the floor with a mop and a bucket near him. The other employee took him to the hospital and the doctors noted that he had a sprained ankle. The church staff had no idea that Joe was not hurt at the church, but because the church had proper worker's compensation coverage, they didn't have any out-of-pocket expenses to pay for Joe's injury. Their worker's compensation insurance premiums did increase the next year but not by enough to hurt the church finances. Eventually it was revealed that Joe never hurt his leg at the church and he was asked to resign. God don't like ugly!

We have discussed a few types of insurance that churches need. The bottom line is that if the church fails to acquire insurance it will pay more in heartache, headache, and out-of-pocket in the long run. Just as important, you need to make sure you and your legal team thoroughly read and understand each insurance policy before signing. Ask questions about statements or clauses that you don't understand. We are so used to just signing paperwork without reading that it could cost the church millions, as it did in the following case.

World Harvest Church v. Grange Mutual Casualty Company

World Harvest Church, led by Pastor Rod Parsley, fought its insurer in court over having to carry the entire burden of a $3.1 million settlement for the beating of a 2-year-old child on its Columbus, Ohio, property.

The case was born out of a settlement World Harvest Church made with Michael and Lacey Faieta, who alleged in a lawsuit that their 2-year-old son was injured when he suffered a "horrific" beating with a ruler by daycare worker Richard Vaughan in 2006.

World Harvest stated at trial that the beating never happened and that the bruises on the child were as a result of a skin rash. However, the jury didn't agree with the church and awarded the family $6 million in damages. The settlement was reduced down to $2.9 million by a judge to reflect limits on damages. World Harvest then settled with the family in 2009 for a sum of $3.1 million, which includes interest since 2006. After the final settlement World Harvest sued their insurance company, Grange Mutual.

At issue was whether the beating of the child falls under corporal punishment or abuse, the latter of which is not covered under World Harvest Church's policy with its former insurer. The case, if decided against World Harvest, would force the church to pay out the full amount on its own.

The trial court sided with World Harvest, and the Tenth District Court of Appeals affirmed the majority of the trial court's decision, finding Grange Mutual had to cover World Harvest for compensatory damage, attorney fees, and post-judgment interest.

However, the Ohio Supreme Court reversed the Tenth Districts judgment that Grange Mutual is responsible for covering the damages. The High Court of Ohio found that the language in the Grange Mutual policy regarding the abuse exclusion bars coverage of World Harvest for an award for damages based on vicarious liability. World Harvest was left carrying the entire debt. Read and understand your insurance policies.

HOW SHOULD YOU TREAT CONTRACTORS AND VENDORS?

"And whatever you do in word or deed, *do* all in the name of the Lord Jesus, giving thanks to God the Father through Him" (Colossians 3:17).

Most churches pay independent contractors/outside consultants for various services from accounting to advertising. Always have a written contract with them spelling out the rights and responsibilities of each party, the duration of the contract and the fact that the contractor is responsible for their own taxes.

Next, make sure that the contract specifically says they are not an employee and refer to the IRS rules concerning who is an employee vs. who is an independent contractor.

Many people want to act as if they are self-employed and receive the entire check. However, when tax time comes, and they didn't put any aside for income tax they want to blame the church for not withholding tax. Avoid this issue up front in the contract.

Make sure the people are really contractors. They should set their own hours, wear what they want (within reason) use their own tools and equipment and the biggest sign is that they have the ability to work for another company or individual and also work for the church.

All churches have **vendors,** from the electric company to the termite inspection company. Make sure you review every invoice because there are lots of checking and invoicing scams that take place daily. If a company that supplies you with goods has an unscrupulous employee they may be sending you falsified invoices and if you are a large church used to paying these type expenses the bill could get paid and you not know about it.

We talked about loyal employees earlier but make sure that if you are using contractors in your financial office they are trustworthy also. There are ways to vet them, and even get referrals. A crooked employee or contractor in your financial business can cause extreme damage.

I know of a case involving a crooked employee that had her innocent boss sent to prison. Although it wasn't a church, the scheme is worth noting because it was so elaborate.

In this case an administrative assistant embezzled thousands of dollars over a five-year period. She was thought to be a loyal employee, but at some point she became disgruntled and greedy. She had a brother that had a maintenance and construction company. The brother's business was failing, so she started writing invoices from the brother's company to her employer; the State of New York.

The invoices would be created stating that the brother's company did work for the State, when in fact he had not done any work. Since the crooked employee had an idea of where work was needed around the department and in other departments, the invoices were believable to the accounting office.

Since the boss was traveling a lot to conduct training all over the state, the administrative assistant would make sure these invoices were paid, often hand delivering them to the accounting office herself.

I'm not sure how the scheme was uncovered but it was revealed that the brother's company received over $340,000 in state funds. The district attorney questioned the woman and she implicated her boss, which had nothing to do with the scheme. However, because the boss was very high-profile in that state, the district attorney saw a chance to use the case to get a promotion. He told the boss that since she should have known that her assistant was embezzling funds she was guilty by association and if she agreed to a plea deal she would be imprisoned for nine months. The executive denied any knowledge or participation, and she refused to agree to a plea deal. The district attorney took the boss to court and had the crooked assistant testify against her. The boss was given a seven-year prison sentence, the assistant received immunity and the district attorney received his promotion.

Be careful that you know everything that is happening in your financial office because you won't be able to trust the legal system to have your back!

The business and financial offices are the hub of the church and should be carefully staffed, guarded and prayed over regularly. These practices will keep your church operating in divine order.

PILLAR TWO

PLANNING TO WIN THE WORLD

What is Strategic Thinking?

"Wisdom rests in the heart of him who has understanding, but what is in the heart of fools is made known" (Proverbs 14:33).

In order to become a strategic leader, you need to first become a strategic thinker. My dad would always answer a question with a question. This made me angry, but his tactic made me become a strategic thinker.

A strategic thinker is someone with the ability to anticipate and envision the future, continue to be flexible, and "turn on a dime" when necessary. A strategic thinker will keep the church on the cutting edge and make sure it's growing and not dying.

Here are some things that experts say make up a strategic thinker,[1] and they are what I believe made me a strategic thinker.

Having a Good Memory

Strategic thinkers are known to have good memories. Some even have photographic memories. For as long as I can remember, I have had a good memory. I was able to use that "elephant" memory to study and make good grades all the way through college and beyond. I used to make up sentences to remember key facts so that I could efficiently study for tests. These sentences had to be something that I would remember—something from my everyday life. For example, in graduate school when learning the attributes of the Godhead that are associated with love, we were taught that they are:

- Benevolence
- Grace
- Mercy
- Persistence

My way of remembering these for the test was to make up a sentence: "Please make beets Gloria." Gloria is my mom, and I used to hate beets, so this is a sentence that I would remember! When the question came up on a test, I would repeat the sentence in my head and remember what each of the first letters stood for. This method of learning led me to graduate with a 4.0 GPA.

Using Imagination

The strategic thinker is a visual thinker. Many pastors are considered visionaries because they see a thing long before it comes to fruition. I know of several visual thinkers that will merely speak a program out of their mouths, and as long as they have the helpers in place to fill in the details, the plan is developed and works perfectly. On example is when a church was trying to find ways to connect and grow. A strategic thinker envisioned having a day where all of the members could get together, outside of a Sunday service, and just have fun. This visionary could see everyone in one area with games for the small children, sports for the older children, board games, food, and fun. The others in the meeting caught the vision and "Family Day" was born. This activity day turned out very well and the members now look forward to it on a quarterly basis.

Using Verbal Thinking

When you think out loud, especially with others, you get a better thought out strategy. Bouncing ideas off others helps you develop a plan from beginning to end. Our ability to talk to ourselves in our heads is limited only by the scope and exactitude of our vocabulary, so talking to yourself is smarter than you think.

Many times when I am having a conversation with good friends or family members about my plans I have to stop and begin writing because I get new ideas to add to the current strategy. I didn't know that I had been doing this just about all my life until at my 50th birthday party my best friend from fourth grade told everyone that we would finish our work early and talk because the teacher was always out of the room. She said, "While we were talking Sherry would often tell me to wait, and then with that little left hand she would start scribbling notes on paper and put the paper in her pocket." I was amazed to hear that, and after she said it, I actually remembered doing that. Everyone, including myself had a good laugh.

I also notice that when I am having conversations with people with similar interests, everyone involved benefits because we share common goals.

If you already possess these thinking skills you are well on your way to becoming a productive leader. If not, don't worry, because these skills can be developed:

- Memorize Scripture.
- Imagine an evangelism excursion to the neighborhood and plan it out.
- Explore what you are feeling about a church project before you think about it.
- Explore financial statements and understand their meaning.
- Talk through a potential church growth program with a fellow pastor.

My parents taught me the game of chess, which I think is the best and first board game that children over six years old should learn. Chess taught me that there are multiple decisions/choices with just as many outcomes. I also learned that once I made a decision, others involved would make decisions, often based on the one I made. When I became a teenager, my father would tell me the choices that I had and the probable outcomes, and I would make decisions based on the results that I desired. This exercise was a part of strategic thinking.

For example, when deciding whether or not I would get a job as a junior in high school, Dad laid out the following scenarios and the pros and cons for each:

1. Get a job and work only weekends and make a little money

2. Get a job and work weekends and after school and make more money
3. Don't get a job and have no money

I weighed these choices out and decided to work after school and on weekends as long as my grades didn't suffer.

Strategic thinking as it relates to the church came into play when our church had a building that needed cleaning and renovating. Instead of throwing away all of the furniture and equipment that was inside, I proposed and was granted permission to clean up the items and have a massive yard sale. I gathered volunteers from all over the church and we spent two weekends sorting and cleaning the usable items and disposing of things that were no longer usable. During the third week, we put the salable items on display and sold almost everything. In the end, we got the building cleaned up and made a decent amount of money in the process.

Each church has members that are willing and able to be strategic thinkers to help the church grow and prosper. Don't be afraid to ask them for help because with strategic thinking and planning we can win the world!

WHAT ARE CHURCH CYCLES OF LIFE?

"To everything there is a season . . . . A time to plant and a time to pluck up what was planted . . . ." (Ecclesiastes 3:1–2).

Here we are in the twenty-first century and everything, including the church, is changing at break-neck speed. A few decades ago most people attended church, and many churches were full every Sunday. But now we have an onslaught of media immorality and family breakdown, and the church doesn't have the skills to handle these rapid changes. This new culture is precisely why we need strategic thinkers—to get the Body of Christ back on the right track!

These days many Americans don't attend church, and many churches are nearly empty week after week. Church closings are occurring at an alarming rate, especially after the economic difficulties of 2008. According to the statistics, several thousand churches are closing every year, and thousands of pastors resign weekly. These churches are often replaced with congregations that want a different, "less demanding" gospel, and leaders/pastors willing to give them what they want. Churches that practice authentic Christianity are becoming a rare breed. We must turn the tide by understanding the problems facing our communities and implement solutions for these changes. These solutions are made up of strategic plans, which are vital to the survival of the church.

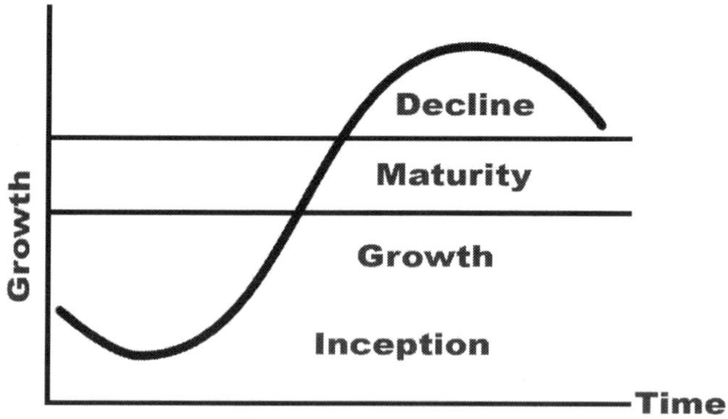

Sigmoid Curve

Before we get into defining a strategic plan, let's talk about the life cycles of most churches. As shown in the "S" curve, also called the Sigmoid Curve; churches start, they grow, they level off, and they begin to deteriorate unless proper measures (strategic plans) are put in place to keep the church alive and thriving.[2]

The first aspect of the Sigmoid Curve is a starting point or the beginnings of a new church. Next, people "bail out" when they see that building a church is hard work, so there is a downward slump before the steady growth. This downward slump is when the glitches are being repaired. This time is full of false starts, dry runs, and "do-overs." This slump or dip is also when people start to learn how to perform within the new plan. They learn to get into a rhythm. Finally, they gather confidence and momentum for growth.

Then there is growth. The growth period could last from several months to several years. This period is when new ministries within the church are formed, and evangelism and outreach are vital priorities for the membership. During the growth period, there is lots of energy and activity, and the church is appealing to the neighborhood and the local community because they are usually very visible.

After the growth period, the church usually hits a plateau. The time of plateau is a time of maturity; when members have been a part of the church for several years and cliques begin to form. I'm not saying that cliques are always bad, but sometimes they are a hindrance for new members because the new people feel that they don't fit in. This hindrance of a clique could be part of the reason for the decline. When the old members get set in their ways and don't accept what "fresh blood" has to suggest, situations can get a little dicey. The children of the older members decide to find "a more modern church" and they leave, as the older members start to die off.

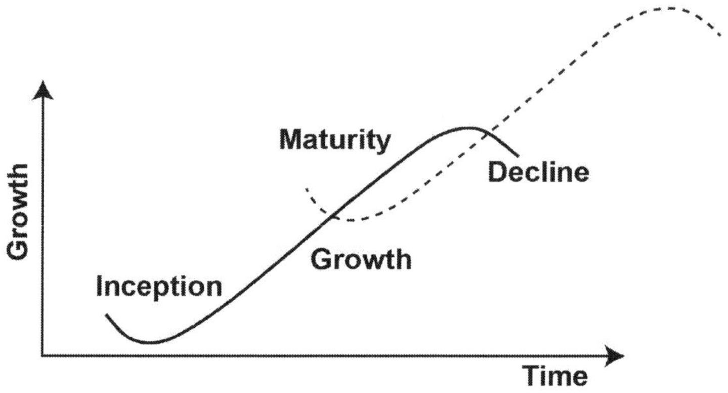

Decline comes next as goals are met and new ones have not been set. During the decline, members fall into a comfort zone, and energy and activity come to a halt or slow down very significantly. Evangelism and outreach are no longer a priority, as members prefer to go to church, feed on the messages, and go home. "This is the way we've always done it," becomes the motto, and membership doesn't realize that the world around them is changing, or they don't care that it has changed. If nothing changes in this church, it will suffer a slow and possibly painful death. Beginning a new cycle before the decline is paramount to maintaining a thriving church. Someone has to have enough insight and horsepower to start the new cycle WHILE THE CHURCH IS STILL GROWING! While the church is still growing leadership has to learn what needs to be accomplished next. That's where the strategic planning comes in!

The church in the diagram above will continue to thrive because while it is still in the growth and maturity stages, it starts a new curve. This church develops strategic plans to revitalize itself, which should be completed every couple of years to avoid decline and death. New ideas, programs, and content to complete the mission of the gospel are the focus here. Ideas such as changing the church's name, adding self-development classes, bringing in new cultures, and even adding younger leaders will help the revitalization process.

There are two key elements that are necessary when creating a strategic plan: an organization ready to be revitalized and a competent leader.

If you don't have people prepared to be revitalized, go through the struggle, think through what's necessary, nothing will change in the organization. The membership has to embrace the change that's coming. There is no avoiding change. The world is changing on a daily basis and as morals decline more effort is needed to keep Jesus at the center of society. If the congregation does not understand the importance of revitalization or is rejecting it, there is no hope for the church.

The church requires a competent leader who can take the organization through the process of growth. You also need courageous followers who can assist in raising the level of competency of a leader (if they are willing). Followers have the opportunity, if the leader is not competent, to help them become competent.[3]

WHAT IS STRATEGIC PLANNING?

"Go to the ant, you sluggard! Consider her ways and be wise" (Proverbs 6:6).

Strategic planning involves a set of decisions and actions utilized to create and implement specific strategies to augment the use of resources and accomplish the organization's goals. The strategy is the plan of action that details how resources should be allocated and what additional internal and external activities to conduct in order to help the organization achieve its goals.

If you want to start or revitalize a church you must have a plan; you must count the cost, you must write the vision and make it plain on paper (Habakkuk 2:2). Many churches and organizations fail because they claim that they are being led entirely by "the Spirit." However, Scripture mandates that we plan (Luke 14:28). Putting ideas, goals, and plans down on paper makes us more committed to making them happen and holds us accountable to those around us.

Christian strategic leaders should base their mission, vision, and organizational model on biblical principles from a Christian world view. We use the Bible as a guide to go forth with the plans that God has given for kingdom advancement. As we ready ourselves for the assignment given by God, we must make sure that we uphold His standard, and His standard requires us to be intentional about everything that we do so that the world won't have a reason to mock Him due to our lack of proper preparation.

Here are three organizational questions that must be asked and answered when planning for revitalization and growth:[4]

Identity Question—Who Are We?

Here we are addressing core values. These are one of the most elusive aspects to discover in the church. Core values can differ from espoused values. Espoused values say, "What do we do?" Preach, teach, give, reach people with the gospel and go on the mission field. These are the things we say that we do. The core values are the actual values. What we **really** do versus what we say we do! When you ask, "Who are we?" be prepared for resistance. That's because some people know that what they say is not what's taking place.

For example, I have audited and reviewed many church accounting systems. The first thing that I do is to have an interview with the business office personnel. This interview consists of an extensive questionnaire that asks what the business staff does on a daily basis and the specific steps they take to accomplish those tasks. When I ask how the funds are collected during Sunday service this process is explained by the business office staff. However, sometimes when I visit the church and observe the collection process during a Sunday service, the procedure described to me during the interview is not the same procedure I observed in person.

Another example that may hit home is when pastors or congregants are asked about their missions' ministry. The church may **say** that they are active in missions, but in reality, they have not gone on a missions trip in years and have not visited the inner city to minister to the homeless either. Foreign and local missions are many times put on the back burner but since many believe they should be a core value of the church, often what is said about their missions activity is not what is actually being done.

Direction Question—Where Are We Going?

Here we are addressing mission and vision. These two set the tone for the future of the church and the ministries within the church. What you need to do is begin at the end, then back up from there to the beginning, then start setting goals and objectives along the way until over time you accomplish what you want. The mission and vision should be well thought out by the leaders and active members of the church so that they will feel a part of the process.

Some churches want to minister strictly to the local community, and some want to reach the homeless. Still, others are led to concentrate on raising up godly families. You have to know your purpose and assignment before moving forward, or confusion will set in quickly, and we know that God is not the author of confusion but of peace (1 Corinthians 14:33).

Strategy Question—How Will We Get There?

Here we are addressing strategy. First, ask God what He wants to be done then get the congregation prepared to begin. Set the strategy formed on biblical principles and a biblical world view. Then move from step to step. This process may take months or years but having it on paper is critical to actually completing the plan.

To formulate a strategy for the church the people involved in this task must integrate their knowledge of the church, its history, environment, vision and mission with the things the church does really well and the activities that make it stand out among other churches. Putting this information to paper will help achieve synergy and create buy-in among the team and the congregation.

SWOT Analysis

In order for a church to create a strategic plan, it first has to know its Strengths, Weaknesses, Opportunities, and Threats. This procedure is called the SWOT analysis.

A cross section of faithful members should complete the SWOT analysis. They should be of all ages and levels of maturity. For example, if you don't have the young adults in on the analysis, you will miss out on a big part of what's going on with the media—for better or worse, but in any case, it's best to be aware.

First, write down everything the group thinks are strengths. This exercise will motivate everyone to see that the church has some great things going on.

Next, write down everything the group thinks are weaknesses. Everyone will not agree at this point. A young person may think that three-hour services are a weakness, but an older person may think that's the perfect length of time. Either way, each person's input should be noted and logged.

Next, the group should write down the opportunities that the church has; in the local area, in the city, the state, the nation, and the world. Some group members may note that a new recreation center opened near the church and there is an opportunity to partner and minister. Another member may notice that lots of communities are starting gardens and the church can attract more members by starting, or participating in, a community garden.

Lastly, the group should be honest in noting the threats to the ministry. This one should be done last because it could potentially kill a good mood and make the atmosphere very somber. Some threats could be an increase in crime in the area, a new church in the area that has a dynamic children's church and the fact that the church building is starting to need repairs that can't be ignored.

The SWOT analysis is a sobering look at where the church is and taking the results seriously will give the church a jump-start on a realistic plan for revitalization and growth.

Writing the Plan

Once the church figures out who they are, where they are going, and how they will get there this information needs to be written down into a strategic plan, with timelines, deadlines, and validation of results. If it isn't written down, it's a bunch of noise, and people will be frustrated because the situation will become blurred by the divergence of individual opinions. Writing the plan stirs accountability in everyone involved and increases the likelihood that the plan will be implemented. It also causes more buy-in by the members that are seeing things improve around the church.

Executing the Plan

Next, the plan has to be executed. After the written plan is set all resources have to be assessed and put in place in the right areas and at the right times to propel the church forward to growth. A timeline and deadlines must be put in place to make sure plans are moving along, even if very slowly. When a member is not completing the tasks given to him or her, the team should first talk to them and if there is no change that member should be asked to step aside and let someone that is willing and able to complete the task take over. I know that feelings can be hurt in the process of executing serious change, but the goal is to revitalize and grow the church and assignments must be where most effective and appropriate for the overall objectives to succeed.

As the plan gets into full gear, a type of synergy will occur because everyone is moving towards the goal of church health. The implementation team is excited, and that excitement flows throughout the church. So, get the plan written and start working it out so that church growth will begin!

Testing the Plan

Once the plan is in action, it has to be tested to be sure that it is going to be effective in the long run. Here are some questions that should be asked while the plan is being implemented and when it is near completion:

1. Does the strategy utilize the opportunities that were noted in the SWOT analysis?
2. Does the strategy eliminate the threats from outside sources that were mentioned in the SWOT analysis and any threats that have surfaced since the beginning of the process?
3. Do the parts of the strategy mesh together to form a whole that is larger than all of its separate parts?
4. Does the strategy demand that the church does what it needs to do to succeed in all of the set goals, the vision and mission?

Overall it is hard to create a strategic plan, but Christ commissioned us to go and win the world, and we can't be flippant in our duty to win souls. The church must regularly implement strategic plans to win souls, make disciples, and keep the physical building up and running to complete the cycle over and over until Jesus comes.

Endnotes

1 Wootton and Horne, Strategic Thinking, 7rate

2 Malphurs, Advanced Strategic Planning, 7ance

3 *Ibid.*, 24.

4 *Ibid.*, 27.

PILLAR THREE

PROTECTING THE PASTOR AND THE CHURCH FROM THE IRS

Why are Pastors Selected for Audit?

"Be sober, be vigilant; because your adversary the devil walks about like a roaring lion, seeking whom he may devour" (1 Peter 5:8).

In my two plus years auditing pastors as an Internal Revenue Agent I learned a lot about the government as well as about churches. First, **the government is BROKE, and they want to get resources from anywhere they can.** They know that the church has special privileges written into law, so they attempt to circumvent those privileges. It takes all but an act of Congress to audit a church because of the perception of separation of church and state (which, by the way, is nowhere in the Constitution). However, instead of auditing the church, the IRS goes in the back door and audits the senior pastor.

If the IRS finds that the pastor's personal tax returns have "irregularities" then they often make a public mockery of him/her and the agent on the case may get cash rewards. IRS agents love to audit ministers and politicians because these high-profile figures can get them promotions if they cash in big on audit adjustments.

If during the audit of a pastor or minister "fraud" is found, not only is that person likely to be brought up on criminal charges and prosecuted but also the agent will have the ammunition needed to request an audit of the church. We will discuss church audits in a later lesson.

When I was an agent I was selected to head up what was loosely called "The Preacher Project." The IRS noticed that there were specific areas of ministers' tax returns that yielded them large sums of money during audits. I received tax returns from all over Georgia and sent the ones with addresses that were far outside Metro Atlanta to various IRS satellite offices for audit. Before I sent a tax return to another city and before I audited the ones from the Atlanta area I tested them for "audit worthiness."

It may come as a shock to you, but the main way a pastor's tax return was selected for audit was because an informant "turned him or her in." Yes, disgruntled congregants or employees would either call in to the 1-800 hotline or write a detailed letter about "what the pastor is up to." If the person called the hotline an IRS employee would try to get the person to reveal their name but if they didn't, the employee would write down all of the information given by the informant.

Once the information from the call was placed on paper or once the letter was secured, that pastor's tax return was pulled and the write-up/letter along with the tax return was sent to me. From there I would read the information and see if the tax return was audit worthy. Audit worthy meant that what the person accused the pastor of would affect the tax return, in that the pastor would owe additional taxes. For example, if the letter accused the pastor of using drugs (which was the case in one of my audits) and that was the only accusation it was not audit worthy unless lots of drugs were involved and his income was not enough to pay for a drug habit. Another example is when the pastor was accused of sleeping with multiple women in the church. Those tax returns were sent back to the IRS service center because that was a God issue and not an IRS issue.

About 98% of the cases that I received were audited. Here are some of the main reasons that Pastors were audited when I was an agent:

- Treating funds received from the church on a weekly basis as non-taxable "love offerings."
- Receiving a small salary but a large housing allowance.
- Not reporting funds from speaking engagements.
- Using church funds for personal endeavors (private inurement).

These were not the only reasons, but these were the most frequent reasons that pastors were audited. Sometimes an informant was happy to leave his or her name, as long as they were assured that the pastor wouldn't find out. Some didn't care if the pastor found out or not. These people often wanted a cash reward. Did you know that when someone "rats out" a pastor or anyone else to the IRS and that audit results in additional tax due, the informant could receive a cash reward? Welcome to the new dystopian world!

When I received cases where an informant was involved the information received by the informant was kept in a pink folder. That pink folder was NEVER to leave my office, so there would be no chance that I mistakenly took information with me that would reveal the identity of the informant. I don't recall the actual number of informant cases that I worked where the informant wanted a cash reward, but it was surely more than one. After I submitted the case for collection I was no longer in the loop to witness whether informants received rewards and how much, but to show you how much incentive the IRS gives informants, here in an excerpt from the IRS regarding informant rewards:

"The IRS Whistleblower Office pays money to people who blow the whistle on persons who fail to pay the tax that they owe. If the IRS uses information provided by the whistleblower, it can award the whistleblower up to 30 percent of the additional tax, penalty and other amounts it collects."[1]

As you can see, if the informant thinks that the pastor has greatly benefited from whatever was reported, there is substantial incentive to let the IRS know about it.

One of the most egregious informant cases that I encountered was when a former church accountant sent a letter to the IRS. Because this man had worked with the church's finances for some time he had a lot of guts to spill. Some of the issues he raised were:

- The pastor's wife never cooked, and they went out to eat every Sunday with funds from that Sunday's offering.
- The pastor and associate pastor went on frequent family vacations using church funds.
- The pastor and associate pastor took church funds and made investments.
- The pastor and associate pastor went to Reno and Las Vegas, Nevada to gamble with church funds, claiming that the wealth of the unrighteous was stored up for the righteous.

Interestingly enough, they won over $10,000 during the Nevada trip. I know this because I pulled a Currency Transaction Report (CTR) on the pastor and the associate pastor and discovered the winnings. Under federal law, banks are required to report any transactions (cash deposits or withdrawals) that total more than $10,000 in any single day to the Treasury. This information is included on a Currency Transaction Report (CTR). The purpose of the CTR is to help the government track large transactions and prevent money laundering.

Needless to say, this case was a mess and I was glad to get it done and turned in to my manager. It came back to haunt me later when, years after I had left the IRS, the pastor attempted to subpoena me in as a hostile witness against the accounting firm that took over after the informant accountant left. The pastor was suing the new accounting firm and somehow my audit, which bled into the time of the new accounting firm, was said to be key to the case. I refused to cooperate, and I never heard from them again.

Pastors should not just depend on others to make sure that their personal houses are in order. They should be proactive in ensuring that all of their financial transactions are above reproach. The slightest indiscretion, like going to the store with the church credit card to get air freshener for the sanctuary but picking up a small flat-screen TV for home at the same time, can break up a congregation.

Make sure that the people doing the accounting at the church and the ones preparing your personal tax returns are above reproach and know what they are doing. To the IRS and to angry congregants and outsiders, ignorance of the rules is no excuse.

Pastors and ministers must be very careful about what they say and do (Ephesians 5:15 NKJV) tells us to walk circumspectly, not as fools but as wise. You are being watched each day that you step out of your home. Make sure what you do glorifies God or the next "Preacher Project" IRS agent out there may be knocking at your door.

WHAT IS PRIVATE INUREMENT?

Private inurement was one of the major issues that I encountered as an IRS agent. Private inurement means that a person or persons at a church are using the church's income or assets to engage in activities that result in the enrichment (make wealthy) of an insider or insiders (such as persons having a personal and private interest in the activities of the church).

Insiders could include the senior pastor, a minister, church board members, officers, and in certain circumstances, employees.

Examples of prohibited inurement include:

- The payment of dividends
- The payment of unreasonable compensation to insiders
- Transferring property to insiders for less than fair market value.[2]

The prohibition against inurement to insiders is absolute; therefore, any amount of inurement is, potentially, grounds for loss of tax-exempt status. In addition, the insider involved may be subject to excise tax or even civil and/or criminal charges.

Private inurement was usually a big problem with small churches when I audited pastors. When there was only a small revenue stream, many times the bulk of it was paid to the pastor, who was attempting to be a full-time pastor. In many cases it would have been better for the pastor to work at least a part-time job to take care of personal expenses. Instead, I have seen the pastor get paid so that he could pay his mortgage or rent while the church lights were cut off.

Excess Economic Benefit

In cases where a church provides an excess economic benefit to an insider, both the church and the insider have participated in an excess benefit transaction. The IRS may levy an excise tax on any insider who illegally benefits from an excess benefit transaction, as well as on church officers who participate in the transaction knowing that it's inappropriate. An insider who benefits from an excess benefit transaction must return the excess benefits to the church.2

For example, if the church needs a new roof they should acquire at least three bids for such a large job. If instead they give the job to one of the deacons, that happens to own a roofing company, they need to be sure that his price is comparable to the prices of other roofing companies in the area. If other roofing companies are charging $5,000 for a roof the size of the church's roof and the deacon is charging $10,000 he is receiving excess economic benefit and must give $5,000 back to the church. In addition, the IRS may charge the deacon and the authorizer of the transaction additional taxes.

Private Interest

In addition, the church's enterprises may not serve the private interests of **any** individual or group. Rather, beneficiaries of a church's activities must be verified objects of charity (such as the poor or the suffering) or the community at large (for example, through the offering of religious services or the sponsoring of religion). Private benefit is different from inurement to insiders. Private benefit may occur even if the beneficiaries are not insiders. Also, private benefit must be significant to jeopardize tax-exempt status.[3]

For example, if the church decides to sponsor a summer youth trip to Florida the trip must be open to all membership and not just the pastor's and elder's children. Also, if the church purchases land from the city and states that the land will be used to build a homeless shelter, the land must not be used to build a private residence or a vacation home to benefit the church leadership.

When the IRS looks at a pastor's personal finances they first want to get a feel for how small or large the church is. Whether the pastor is full-time (has no additional job) or part-time (has a full-time job outside of pastoring) questions concerning the size of the church are asked during the initial interview. If an agent determines that the church is small, and the pastor does not have a job or additional non-church related income, they will look closely for private inurement. Although the agent can't ask for the church books and records, usually the pastor's personal books and records will reveal what's going on at his small church.

For example, I once audited a minister that felt that the Lord told him to quit his job and go into full time ministry. Up to that point he was renting a small building and had a congregation of about 50 people. He felt that in order to grow he needed to quit his full-time job and devote all of his efforts to the ministry. Soon, funds begin to be tight as church bills and personal bills needed attention. His wife worked but her income was not enough to take care of all of the household income, and the pastor was not including the funds from the church as taxable income. I received an anonymous letter with his tax return. The letter said that the informant had recently left the church and that the pastor was, "using all of the church money to pay his personal expenses." That statement was not totally true, but because a substantial amount of the funds received from the church were going to meet the pastors personal expenses he was denied these funds as a housing allowance and they were deemed taxable income.

When the church is larger and the revenue stream is stronger and steady, there is more temptation for a pastor to spend more on things that he or she has always wanted. I have seen pastors use church funds to pay for not only their own automobiles but their wives and college aged children. Neither the wife nor the children worked at the church, so private inurement was a definite finding.

My very first pastoral audit was of a medium sized church in Metro Atlanta. The pastor was said to be a good motivational speaker and storyteller, and he had a faithful congregation. This tax return was selected because the informant was angry about the pastor's high standard of living. The pastor, his wife, and son were all driving luxury vehicles, but he was the only one working at the church. The son was attending a private college on top of that.

I reviewed the tax return, remembering the information in the pink folder that I left in my office. The pastor had no salary on the tax return. He had a Schedule C, "Profit or Loss from Business." I asked the pastor what business he was running, and he said that the funds on that schedule were from his speaking engagements. The amount was under $20,000. I looked all through the tax return and that amount was the only income reported. He had travel and other expenses that reduced that figure down to a net income of under $10,000.

During the initial interview I asked the pastor about his family, his home, his cars and his other sources of income. He confirmed that there were three luxury cars and college tuition. He also confirmed that he didn't have a job or any other sources of income.

I then asked him how he paid for his home, the cars, and the private college tuition. He told me he used his earnings from being a pastor. I told him that he couldn't possibly pay for all of that with a net income, per the tax return, of under $10,000. I asked him did he receive a salary or any other funds from the church. Then it came out. He said, "Yes, I get money every Sunday from the church offerings but that is a love gift!" This pastor was receiving funds every Sunday and using those funds to pay for his personal lifestyle but thinking these funds were not taxable.

He experienced a rude awakening when I informed him that those Sunday funds were taxable and that the audit had to be expanded to all three open years so that I could determine how much in "love gifts" he was receiving each year. His final tax bill was substantial but at least 5 years after that first audit he was still senior pastor at that church, so I suppose it didn't hurt his reputation at that church if they ever found out.

One other church put the pastor out and changed the locks because the board said he was improperly handling church funds. By the time I received the case it was a full-blown mess. This pastor was very proud and treated me like some type of underling. Although it made me angry I had to keep my composure and not lash out. He ended up with a large bill also. However, he went and started a new church, with some of the loyal congregants. I heard tell that he had a large fundraiser for his tax bill. But since I had already left the IRS by that time I wouldn't know if he included those funds on his personal tax return.

HOW CAN THE PASTOR AVOID A PERSONAL AUDIT?

The federal government is becoming bolder in its scrutiny of the church. Within the last decade Congress has called for the investigation of several large ministries, sitting irregularities in the operation of ministry. Although several of the ministries rightfully refused to disclose church operations there is still a tendency of the government to attempt to interfere in church affairs because the church currently brings in billions of dollars that the government can't touch.

Because of the temptation to acquire church funds the IRS has found a back door into the investigation of ministry operations. They are now increasing the number of audits performed on senior pastors and other ministry gifts. Since they have a hard time gaining permission to audit churches they have begun auditing the senior pastors of churches of all sizes, and if they find that the pastor's tax return has major audit adjustments, including private inurement, they will try to get permission to audit the church.

When I was a revenue agent, I was placed in charge of what was loosely called the "Preacher Project." Two women in a

Midwest IRS office were putting together a guide to audit pastors and ministers under an IRS program called the Market Segment Specialization Program, or MSSP for short and I was coordinating with them as I audited ministers in the Atlanta area. This program, which is currently in full force, spells out several areas that the IRS has noted abuse" on pastor's personal tax returns. When a pastor is audited, whether it is from an informant contacting the IRS or some other method of selection, several areas are heavily scrutinized. Here, I will discuss a few of the top areas and explain how to possibly get the revenue agent to send the pastor's file back to the service center (back to storage) because it is not audit worthy. In an earlier section of this book I noted that "audit worthy" means there is something on the tax return that would cause the revenue agent to proceed with an audit of the tax return. IRS agents don't like to spend lots of time reviewing tax returns that won't yield any additional tax, so the goal is to have the tax return deemed unworthy of audit. I can't guarantee that by following the steps outlined below the tax return won't be audited but following the procedures will make it easier for the IRS to just skip the pastor's tax return and move on to greener pastures.

(This information below is predicated on the fact that the pastor has already been properly identified as a minister based on the IRS guidelines).

The Structure of the Pastor's Pay

Although most senior pastors are treated as employees and receive W-2's there are some pastors that either only receive cash payments from the weekly offerings or receive cash payments in addition to paychecks that generate W-2's. These pastors call this payment a "love offering" and they believe that these funds are non-taxable gifts. This was the case in my very first pastor audit and I assessed over $20,000 in additional tax because the pastor was not reporting the funds that he received straight from the offering baskets every Sunday that he wasn't out speaking.

The IRS sees the "love offering" as taxable income, so instead of receiving cash from the offerings the pastor should receive a salary that is designated by the board of directors and that is reflected on a W-2 each year. Any additional funds received by the pastor from the church should be well documented as reimbursement or taxable and should be added to the W-2 if they are taxable. That way there will be no question that the pastor reported all taxable income.

The Housing Allowance

Not only does the pastor's housing allowance require approval by a board of directors; it has to be reasonable and be the lesser of rental value, actual expenses, or the board-approved amount. As an IRS agent, I witnessed cases in which the board of directors did not approve the housing allowance; sometimes because there was not a board of directors or any governing body. In all of the cases the housing allowance was very high and sometimes even more than the pastor's salary. If the IRS sees that the salary is less than the housing allowance, even if the amount given to the pastor equals the actual expenses, it will be reduced to at least that salary amount. The IRS has said that if a pastor is only worth that salary amount then his or her housing allowance shouldn't be more. To avoid an audit based on housing allowance the pastor must make sure that the calculation of self-employment tax on the housing allowance is clearly stated on the tax return. When looking at a senior pastor's tax return, a revenue agent is going to make an educated guess as to whether the pastor received a housing allowance and if the agent determines that the pastor probably received housing, he or she will look for the self-employment tax calculation. The educated guess will consist of the agent reviewing the church website and going on the Internet to see where the pastor lives, among other things. If the pastor lives in a luxury home, it will be assumed that the church is issuing a housing allowance.

Private Inurement

Private inurement is a big issue and can make the pastor's face show up on television and in newspapers. Many times, pastors receive large sums of money or lavish gifts, like private jets, that cause the eyebrows of everyday working people and the government to be raised. If the pastor is receiving large amounts of money and putting the church into financial bondage, then the IRS will make a big deal of this perceived extravagance and audit the pastor.

When I was a revenue agent auditing ministers, I regularly saw the senior pastor of small churches receiving over 50% of the church's weekly or monthly income. Some of the churches were having trouble keeping the lights on. I knew this because the church's finances were comingled with the pastor's personal finances. Commingling means mixing together or combining. This occurs when the pastor and/or family members are handling the church finances. In some cases when reviewing the pastor's personal canceled checks, I saw the church's utility bill payments. When I asked why the pastor had to pay the utility bills sometimes the church was just starting, and the pastor was using funds from his full-time job to rent a building and pay utilities. Other times the pastor had taken the bulk of the offerings and, when the utility bills were due, he had to pay them with funds that were in his personal account. The worse thing a pastor can do is commingle church and personal funds. When a revenue agent sees or suspects commingling it's open season and the pastor will likely be audited for all open years, meaning for the last three years of tax returns.

Here are some of the ways that I detected private inurement when I was a revenue agent:

- Flipping through the pastor's personal canceled checks to see what was paid.
- Comparing the pastor's expenses to his reported income to see if expenses were significantly more than income.
- Checking property records to see who paid for personal property.
- Driving by the church to see if the church was being neglected while the pastor lived in luxury housing and drove a luxury car.
- Checking to see if the pastor's spouse or other family members were being paid in any way by the church, and if so for what duties.

- Asking for the housing designation letter if the pastor indicated that he or she received a housing allowance.
- Asking for invoices for some of the pastor's personal purchases to see if the church made the purchase.
- Checking the pastor's personal credit card statements for travel and checking to see if the church paid the credit card bills.
- Checking the pastor's bank statements for unusual deposits and inquiring about the source of the funds.
- Go on the Internet to look up information about the pastor and the church to see if anyone was complaining about the pastor. (Internet was not as big back then, but I am sure that this is a well-used source of information for revenue agents these days).

To try and avoid an audit based on private inurement:

- Keep church and personal finances separate.
- Have a designated salary and get paid with church checks.
- Have the church issue a W-2 annually.
- Do not commingle church and personal funds.
- Make sure that any housing allowance is properly designated.
- Do not have the church pay relatives that are not actually working at the church.
- If relatives are church employees make sure their salaries are comparable to the marketplace and not extravagant.

- Do not have the church pay for maid service or a personal valet.
- Do not enter into real estate transactions involving the church and the pastor's personal real estate.
- Do not purchase church assets at a discount or sell the church personal assets at over market value prices.
- Do not obtain loans from the church. If you have obtained a loan from the church be sure it has a set repayment date and a set interest rate.

Other Ways to Avoid a Personal Audit

Aside from the above areas that are chosen for review during a pastor's audit, pastors should be aware that their actions in the pulpit could also trigger an audit. I don't believe that any pastor should be afraid to speak what, "thus saith the Lord" from the pulpit. Nevertheless, pastors need to note that the congregation is full of different kinds of people.

Your members and regular visitors are there to hear what the Lord has for them. But others may have ulterior motives. If a pastor starts to be well known for being politically incorrect then politicians, government agents or even people that strongly oppose the pastor's views may show up. Some of these people will report back to the government or the heads of their groups. Others may attempt to disrupt the service if you are speaking out concerning a volatile topic. For example, several homosexuals have infiltrated churches that publicly call homosexuality a sin. In the middle of service these "special guests" have stood up and started cursing, kissing, and even performing sexual acts. These people were eventually escorted out of the church and in some instances the police were called.

Some of the pastors were reported to the IRS because the antagonists wanted the government to audit the pastors and strip the churches of their tax-exempt status for speaking out.

My personal opinion is that the churches should not oppose the termination of the government given *501(c)(3)* because a church is tax immune and can't be taxed with or without that status. However, many churches are afraid of losing the *501(c)(3),* thus they remain silent of critical issues.

Now that I am off my soapbox, here are some additional areas to avoid if you want to avoid a personal audit of the pastor's tax return.

- "Hate speech" is a hot button these days. Be firm and don't change your message but don't conduct witch-hunts of those that are living a sinful lifestyle.
- Don't endorse candidates in the name of the church because a church can't endorse a candidate. The pastor, in his/her personal capacity, can endorse anyone he/she wants to.
- Don't use church funds to give to political candidates or groups that are anti-government.
- Don't let candidates stand up in the pulpit and solicit funds.

- Don't let fringe groups or their leaders act on behalf of the church, speak at the church, or use the church as validation for their cause.

WHAT IF THE IRS SELECTS THE PASTOR FOR AUDIT?

Under the unfortunate circumstance in which the pastor is selected for audit there are several steps that, if put in place, can minimize financial and social impact.

If the pastor is selected for audit it is my belief that he or she should not meet with the IRS. The pastor should select a competent attorney or CPA to represent him or her and funnel all information and documentation through this person via a Power of Attorney. Using a representative will help shield the pastor from a potential atheistic or antagonistic revenue agent. We have to remember that not everyone likes Christians and some people are hostile toward Christian leaders. For example, a revenue agent that was abused by a priest in the past may try to retaliate through the audit of a pastor.

Why Hire a Representative for the Audit?

Another important reason to hire a representative is because IRS agents and auditors take advantage of taxpayers that attend audits alone. They may try to disallow all of your deductions, even if you have canceled checks and invoices. However, with a CPA or attorney handling your case it would be less likely that they would be so bold.

In addition, another good thing about hiring an experienced representative is that they know the tricky questions that IRS agents ask during the initial interview and can stop the pastor from talking his or her way into additional taxes.

For example, in the initial interview one of the questions the agent/auditor will ask is if you received any insurance or inheritance money during the year being audited. If you say yes you will have to prove that you received the insurance funds. But let's say you forgot about a car accident you had in January in which you received $3,500 from the person's insurance company. If you say that you didn't receive insurance funds, the auditor will include that money as unreported income when they see that deposit on the bank statement and it doesn't match with your regular income patterns. A good representative will be able to rebut this income addition and help you avoid tripping up during other "trick questions."

I had a case where I was auditing a company in which a woman embezzled thousands of dollars over a five-year period. She was the accountant at a small business and the company checks came in duplicate, with some type of carbon paper in between. She would type out checks to one of the vendors, like the power company, type backwards over the top check with correction tape so the top check was now blank, separate the check and the duplicate then type her name or some other name on the original. She would take the duplicate, the one that had the power company's name on it, and place it in the file cabinet with the invoice that the power company sent. Later she would write a real check to the power company. The owner was making good money and didn't even realize that his expenses, per the bookkeeping software, were extra high. In fact, they were double since she would have two checks/payments for each invoice, one was a real payment and one where the actual check was made out to her or some jewelry shop or department store where she bought lavish goods.

This woman got sick and had to be placed in the hospital. She apologized profusely to the owner and asked the company secretary to bring the bookkeeping to the hospital so that she could do her job while she recovered, and they complied! But she eventually couldn't keep up with her scheme the second time she had to go into the hospital. The owner got a call from a vendor that said they weren't paid. The owner went into the files and found the invoice and the duplicate check and told the vendor the check number of the payment.

The vendor stated that they received no such payment. The owner then went and found the actual bank statements and noted that the check number for that vendor payment was actually cleared as a check to a department store. He told me that he spent the next 9 hours straight, going through all of the bank statements trying to match up duplicate checks with the actual checks.

The woman had hidden the actual checks but there were copies of the cleared checks in the bank statements. Hundreds of thousands of dollars later he had to decide whether to prosecute. He decided not to prosecute because the woman's husband said they would pay the company back.

I ended up picking the woman's tax returns for audit because I knew she and her husband's income was under reported due to the money she embezzled. Her husband hired a representative and this man really did them justice. He met me at every turn with answers that helped his client. He was able to show that deposits were made with money that came from other bank account withdrawals, so I was not able to make all of the extra deposited funds "income." He also proved that the couple had gifts and other money deposited that was not considered income.

The couple ended up owing back a lot of money, but their additional tax would have been at least $30,000 more if they had not had the proper representation because revenue agents are not taught to dig deeper to help the taxpayer.

As a side note, because the company decided not to prosecute the woman she was able to go to work as a bookkeeper for another company that was never told what she had done.

Choosing a Representative

In selecting a representative try to select one that's even-tempered; one that won't be hostile to the IRS employee or try to make the IRS employee feel incompetent. Selecting a jerk usually results in more money being extracted from you.

Once I audited a business that used an attorney as their representative. Upon entering this attorney's office, I immediately noticed that he was very self-absorbed and condescending towards me. One complete wall of his office was a collage of newspaper clippings that mentioned his name. For example, if there was a client that he represented for some serious crime and he won the case, he had that headline on the wall. This was not just a collection of newspaper clippings pinned up on the wall via thumbtacks—this was a professionally created art piece of all of his legal accomplishments. During the audit, while I was trying to ascertain his client's information and status, he kept going on about cases he had won. I think he wanted me to feel intimidated but instead my "something is very wrong here" radar started to alarm loudly inside my head. A few years later that notable lawyer was convicted and put in prison for conspiring with two other men to kill his wife. Although I am very hard to intimidate, he made it hard to be fair to his client because of his pompous attitude.

The bottom line is to make sure you trust the person that you let stand in front of the IRS on your behalf. Make sure they are firm but not combative.

Preparing for a Speedy Audit

Once a representative is selected the tax return in question and all supporting documentation should be gathered. Have your selected representative examine the entire tax return and the documentation. Every number on that tax return came from somewhere. If you didn't keep good records you need to immediately start gathering receipts and calling vendors, utility companies, and banks for replacement copies of invoices and statements.

Then gather all of the applicable records, categorize them, and place them in the proper folders.

For example, income . . . if the pastor had church income and income from rental real estate, the W-2 from the church should be placed in one folder and the documentation of rental earnings in a separate folder.

Usually when a pastor's tax return is selected for audit the IRS has selected specific information to verify. For example, if your travel meals and entertainment deduction appear high based on their current computer-generated formula, the letter that you receive from the revenue agent will ask for all books and records used to determine the travel meals and entertainment expense deduction.

Place all of the requested expense verifications in separate files. If the agent asked for documentation of your automobile mileage you should have a folder with a calendar for that year showing all of your church related travel, the mileage for those trips and all parking and toll receipts. Prayerfully the receipts and other documentation in your folders match the numbers on the tax return. That way the revenue agent will be out of your life as quickly as possible.

The revenue agent will always ask for all of your bank statements so make sure you and your representative have reviewed the banks statements and written down explanations for any unusual transactions; like large deposits, large withdrawals, and international transactions. When the questions come up you want a ready answer to let the agent know that your tax return is clean and not full of audit adjustments.

Place non-requested expense documentation in separate files also, but make sure that your representative doesn't give these extra files to the agent. IRS agents and auditors almost always ask for additional information after the audit has started. You want to have the information handy if they ask for it, but you do not want to give it to them if they have not asked for it; giving them license to go on a fishing expedition with your records.

What About Missing Records?

If you have receipts missing there are ways to reconstruct these expenses. We already mentioned contacting the businesses and individuals you paid, to see if they have copies of the receipts. There are also other ways to reconstruct expenses.

If you are a pastor, especially one in full-time ministry, logic dictates that you have expenses associated with ministry. Many pastors also have side businesses, and if they have income from those businesses logic dictates that they have expenses associated with that income.

Under what's called "the Cohan Rule" you can argue for the inclusion of your expenses during an audit. The Cohan Rule derives from an excellent old federal court decision. Mr. George M. Cohan, a famous New York theatrical celebrity, brought this court case against the IRS in the early 20th century. Mr. Cohan was on the go a lot and when he got audited he didn't have many of his hotel, cab, and tip documentation. The IRS uses Internal Revenue Code Section 162—Ordinary and Necessary Business Expenses, to disallow expenses that aren't documented, and Mr. Cohan challenged them due to the nature of his work. Mr. Cohan won the case, giving you the right to reconstruct records and write down some expenses based on your recollection. This can't be abused though; you have to have some documents handy.

When I was an Internal Revenue Agent we were told that if the taxpayer had at least 80% of his or her records go ahead and allow the other undocumented but explained 20% under the Cohan Rule. Never let an IRS agent/auditor tell you that because you don't have some records you are disallowed the expense.

Here's an example of use of the Cohan Rule: If you have a mileage deduction on the tax return but you can't find your entire mileage log, you can use the fourth or half of the log you do have and extrapolate it over the whole year. For example, if you can only find three months of mileage logs and for those three months you drove 1,000 business/ministry miles, you can safely use 4,000 (1,000 times 4 quarters) as your annual business/ministry miles under the Cohan Rule. Thank you Mr. Cohan!

Having an impending audit handled quickly and thoroughly can also keep the pastor out of the media. Pastors are one of the high-profile groups that IRS agents like to audit because if they come up with serious audit adjustments the pastor may be prosecuted, and the lead agent could receive awards and maybe even a promotion. So, when an audit is swiftly shut down the chances of the pastor being raked over the coals by the media is slim to none. It's better to put out the flame of the IRS than to do damage control because the pastor was not prepared to handle an audit!

HOW CAN THE IRS AUDIT A CHURCH?

Congress has instituted special restrictions, found in IRC Section 7611, on how and when the IRS may execute civil tax inquiries and examinations of churches. The IRS may only launch a church tax inquiry if an applicable high-level Treasury Department official judiciously believes, based on a written statement of the facts and circumstances, that the church: (a) may not qualify for the exemption or (b) may not be paying tax on an unrelated business or other taxable activity.

Constraints on Church Inquiries and Examinations

Restrictions on questioning and examinations of church books and records apply only to churches (including organizations claiming to be churches if such status has been recognized by the IRS) and conventions or associations of churches. They don't apply to related persons or organizations. Thus, for example, the rules don't apply to schools that, although operated by a church, are organized as separate legal entities. Similarly, the rules don't apply to integrated auxiliaries of a church.

Regulations concerning church investigations and examinations do not apply to all church inquiries by the IRS. The most common exception relates to routine requests for information. For example, IRS requests for information from churches about filing of returns, compliance with income or Social Security and Medicare tax withholding requirements, supplemental information needed to process returns or applications and other similar inquiries are not covered by the special church audit rules.

Restrictions on church inquiries and examinations don't apply to criminal investigations or to investigations of the tax liability of any person connected with the church, such as a contributor or minister. This is how they are able to get into the church records though criminal investigation of a church leader.

The procedures of IRC Section 7611 will be used in initiating and conducting any inquiry or examination into whether an excess benefit transaction (as that term is used in IRC Section 4958) has occurred between a church and an insider. Once the pastor or a person that had direct access to the finances is audited and irregularities are found, the IRS agent writes a formal request to examine the church records.

During my years auditing pastors, I never had the occasion to write the upper management about auditing a church. However, I was privy to information about a church audit that was started in the Midwest. The pastor of a large church was audited, and the IRS agent found that the pastor had signature rights on several church bank accounts. The agent was able to trace deposits in the pastor's personal accounts to checks he had written from church accounts. These deposits were not included in the pastor's income nor were they salary. The amount was substantial, and the agent, after meeting with his manager, decided to send the pastor's case to the criminal investigation division and that a letter asking for permission to audit the church was in order. The letter went up the chain and the church was audited. The audit found that the pastor and a few other leaders were virtually living high off of the church funds and not much real ministry was being achieved. This was a blight on the church, as are all cases of this nature.

Church Audits Based on Free Speech

If the church is a *501(c)(3)* does the pastor have to keep silent on some matters?

Sometimes you may hear of a pastor that preaches fire and brimstone. A pastor that is not afraid to preach about hard, politically incorrect subjects may be setting the church up for an audit.

When a pastor is strong enough to challenge the culture and the public policy of the day by speaking out against things deemed ungodly in the Bible, he surely ruffles feathers. People that don't like the truth of the word of God and don't want the conviction of the Holy Spirit may go to the government and turn that church in with the propose of having it stripped of its tax-exempt status. According to law and policy, a tax-exempt organization, including the church, has to align with public policy over its values and beliefs.

Churches that are tax-exempt and incorporated are constantly at risk of severe government intrusion when they go against the grain of the culture.

Review these court case excerpts concerning churches:

. . . Upon the other hand, the corporation is a creature of the State. It is presumed to be incorporated for the benefit of the public. It receives certain special privileges and franchises, and holds them subject to the laws of the State and the limitations of its charter. Its powers

are limited by law. It can make no contract not authorized by its charter. Its rights to act as a corporation are only preserved to it so long as it obeys the laws of its creation.
Hale v. Henkel, 201 US 43 at 74 (1906)

Appellants appeal on the basis that the circuit court had no authority over them because they are a recognized religious organization, a church. On first reflection they appeared to be correct but upon closer study of the complaint and the judgment we are of the opinion that this is not an improper interference by the government into a church, or ecclesiastical, matter. When the members of the church decided to incorporate their body under the laws of the state of Florida they submitted themselves to the jurisdiction of the state courts in all matters of a corporate nature, such as accounting for funds.
Matthews v. Adams 520 So. 2d 334 (1988)

The Court asserts that an exempt organization must "demonstrably serve and be in harmony with the public interest," must have a purpose that comports with "the common community conscience," and must not act in a manner "affirmatively at odds with the declared position of the whole Government." Taken together, these passages suggest that the primary function of a tax-exempt organization is to act on behalf of the Government in carrying out governmentally approved policies.
Bob Jones University v. United States, 461 US 574 at 585 (1983)

These and other cases are proof that the state will use its power against a church when it wants to.

The Audit Process

The IRS has set forth formal procedures for auditing a church. The sequence of the audit process is:

1. If the reasonable belief requirement is met, the IRS must begin an inquiry by providing a church with written notice containing an explanation of its concerns.
2. The church is allowed a reasonable period in which to respond by furnishing a written explanation to alleviate IRS concerns.
3. If the church fails to respond within the required time, or if its response is not sufficient to alleviate IRS concerns, the IRS may, generally within 90 days, issue a second notice, informing the church of the need to examine its books and records.
4. After issuance of a second notice, but before commencement of an examination of its books and records, the church may request a conference with an IRS official to discuss IRS concerns. The second notice will contain a copy of all documents collected or prepared by the IRS for use in the examination and subject to disclosure under the Freedom of Information Act, as supplemented by *IRC Section 6103* relating to disclosure and confidentiality of tax return information.
5. Generally, examination of a church's books and records must be completed within two years from the date of the second notice from the IRS.

If at any time during the inquiry process the church supplies information sufficient to alleviate the concerns of the IRS, the matter will be closed without examination of the church's books and records. There are additional safeguards for the protection of churches under IRC Section 7611. For example, the IRS can't begin a subsequent examination of a church for a five-year period unless the previous examination resulted in a revocation, notice of deficiency, or assessment or a request for a significant change in church operations, including a significant change in accounting practices.

Avoiding a Church Audit

As I stated before, the U.S. government is broke and looking for money in every corner. Also, there are atheists and others that are lobbying for the church's special privileges to be taken away. They want the church to pay real estate taxes on the church building, they want the pastor to pay income tax on the housing allowance and they want the church to pay tax on the tithes and offerings received by congregants!

Because of this animosity towards the church, now more than ever the pastor and leaders must make sure to protect the church from IRS scrutiny. Proper accounting for church finances is paramount. Policies and procedures must be put in place that ensure proper separation of duties in the financial office, and that no private inurement or private benefit takes place. The pastor and leaders that have anything to do with the church's finances need to be sure that their personal finances are in order, are totally separate from the church's finances and that they have a competent accountant to prepare their personal tax returns. These measures will help to ensure that the IRS stays away from the churches financial business.

Endnotes

1 Publication1828.pdf.o

2 *Ibid.*

3 *Ibid.*

PILLAR FOUR

PREVENTING MINISTERIAL AND PASTORAL PROSECUTION

Why is it Important to Know Our Legal Culture?

A lawsuit against the church, whether filled with factual information or lies, can be the death of that church. It is imperative that the pastor and church leaders do all in their power to avoid any of the churches business being made public. As I declare in the training on ***Pastors & Ministers Audits,*** the IRS loves to have clergy in the news because, when I was an IRS agent, the agents involved look forward to monetary awards and promotions for exposing the Church. Many IRS employees are anti-Christian and they will do all that they can to discredit the name of Christ, so let's make sure we don't leave that door open.

The information in this book was created in collaboration with other experts on church matters. Because of the sensitivity of the information being shared, the names of my colleagues and the names of specific pastors and churches will be changed or omitted. Some generic names will be used to help with the flow of the examples. The final chapter of this book was written by my friend and tax attorney, Nathan MacPherson, who is not only a good Christian man but a defender of the faith and of Christian pastors that find themselves in legal turmoil.

Here is a little about my other colleagues.

One of the contributors is a lawyer with over 25 years of experience. He received his undergraduate degree from Harvard University and his Juris Doctorate from the University of California at Berkeley. He has represented plaintiffs and defendants in several cases involving churches and pastors.

The other contributors are current and retired law enforcement officers from local counties and cities in the Metro Atlanta area. They have extensive experience with churches and the type of cases that often arise in the church.

Separation of Church and State/Government

Federal and State laws are constructed to stay out of church business. In the case of Christianity, the courts will not make decisions on behalf of or against the Bible. For example, the Supreme Court of Georgia, in Anderson v. Dowd, 268 Ga. 146 (1997), ruled:

> The constitutional guarantee of freedom of religion "encompasses the "power (of religious bodies) to decide for themselves, free from state interference, matters of church

> government as well as those of faith and doctrine.'" [Cit.] "First Born Church of the Living God v. Hill, 267 Ga. 633, 634 (1) (481 S.E.2d 221) (1997). Thus, civil courts have no jurisdiction to inquire into and to control the acts of the governing authority of a religious organization undertaken with reference to its internal affairs. Tucker v. Paulk 148 Ga. 228, 229 (2) (96 S.E. 339) (1918).

With that said, it's to the detriment of the church when situations get out of hand and the world/courts are sought after to solve the problems of the people of God. The late Frances Schaeffer, in his book, *The Mark of the Christian,* posits:

> The church is to be a loving church in a dying culture. How, then, is the dying culture going to consider us? Jesus says, "By this shall all men know that ye are my disciples, if ye have love one to another." In the midst of the world, in the midst of our present dying culture, Jesus is giving a right to the world. Upon his authority he gives the world the right to judge whether you and I are born-again Christians on the basis of our observable love toward all Christians.

So, when the church is fighting within its local body or churches are fighting other churches or members are fighting members and these issues are brought to the world to judge, we are telling the world that we don't belong to

Jesus. We must work to avoid these conflicts and disputes on the front end, and if we can't avoid them we must take proper, biblical steps to resolve the issues without letting the world judge us. The following chapters contain some of the issues that get the church entangled in lawsuits that bring the world into the church's business and make a mockery of the Body of Christ.

POWER STRUGGLES IN THE CHURCH

New Wine in Old Wineskins

Greenlakes Church was excited about receiving their new pastor. They had been searching for ten months and had finally found the candidate that best fit their culture. Pastor Bailey was middle-aged—not too young and not too old. He was dynamic but full of wisdom. An added benefit to selecting pastor Bailey was that Mrs. Bailey had an accounting degree and would be leaving her full-time job to help her husband with the ministry.

The Baileys arrived and the welcome celebration and dinner went well, but now it was time to get down to business. For the first week pastor Bailey, who was Greenlakes' first full-time pastor, reviewed all of the church policies and finances during the day and met with the trustees each evening to ask questions about how things ran and to discuss church growth plans. After three weeks everything was starting to gel. The financial offices acquired a new software program to better account for the weekly giving, the security system was upgraded to protect the four staff members that were at the church during the day, and the sign outside the church received an upgrade to attract new members. The seasoned members were pleased with the improvements and with Pastor Bailey's sermons.

Then came the time for the monthly board of trustees meeting. The meeting was always on the first Tuesday night of the month and the chairman of the board, Mr. Wesley, took out his Wells Fargo church debit card to buy some snacks for the meeting. When he got to the cashier the card was denied. He thought that was strange, but he paid for the snacks out of his pocket and left the store; knowing that he could just get a cash reimbursement once he reached the church.

Upon arrival at the meeting Mr. Wesley was confused because eleven people were sitting in the conference room and the board was made up of only five people. He introduced himself as chairman of the trustee board and asked why these people, whom he had recently started seeing at Sunday services, were there. To his surprise, and the shock of the other four regular board members, the six new people introduced themselves as new board members. Mr. Wesley proclaimed that he had not authorized any new members and the other four members agreed. However, Pastor Bailey walked in and made a speech.

"Good evening everyone. Welcome to the new Greenlakes Christian Church board of directors. We have six new board members: Dr. Saddler, attorney Daniels, Dr. Luckett, Chief Taylor, Mrs. Crain, and Mrs. Bailey. They have all moved here to Atlanta with me from Miami and will be helping to build the church."

As the old board members sucked all of the air out of the room Mr. Wesley stood up in protest. "What do you think you're doing? We elected you to be the pastor and preach, not to turn the church upside down!" Pastor Bailey responded, "Be certain that I am trying to improve the church and grow it. I have been researching this church since I received the invitation to interview. It has been stagnant for several years and is on the path to decline. I took this position as a challenge to revive the church. I have enacted new systems that will help boost membership, account for the finances, and get the church in order. Mrs. Crain and Mrs. Bailey will manage the bank accounts and finances from now on and they will be the two signers, Chief Taylor and Dr. Saddler will be in charge of counting and depositing the giving, and Dr. Luckett and attorney Daniels will work on upgrades to the church policies and procedures. All of you can select which area you would like to join in. I am really excited about the growth that will occur as we implement these upgrades."

The old board members were speechless. Then one of them said, "You can't do this! You have no right. Who gave you the authority to come in here and make all these changes? All five of us have been at this church for over 20 years and now you think you can just come in here and upset the apple cart?"

The original five members of the board of trustees ended up filing a lawsuit against Pastor Bailey the next day. They were livid that he would make all of these changes without even a peep or a courtesy call to them. They obtained a lawyer, a friend of Mr. Wesley, and Pastor Bailey also obtained counsel—a friend of attorney Daniels.

All involved had the good sense to keep the matter low-key and go on with services as usual, but there were no board meetings during the development of the case, and the old board of trustees did not participate in any activities outside of showing up for Sunday and Wednesday service. Pastor Bailey figured they showed up to try to collect evidence against him for court, but he just preached as he usually did, and most members didn't know anything was afoot.

Four months later, after each side requested and obtained discovery (information and answers to questions given to each party in a lawsuit), it was time for the first hearing before the judge. The Judge, Joseph Dane, was only interested in hearing the opening arguments and reviewing the church bylaws. Although the lawyers were not surprised, the trustees and Pastor Bailey were stunned when Judge Dane said, "We will have a one-hour recess and I will be ready to render a decision in this case after that hour is over." "What could that mean?" stated Mr. Wesley to the handful of church members that bothered to attend the hearing. They just shrugged their shoulders and left the courtroom. Pastor Bailey asked his lawyer the same question and his lawyer smiled and said, "You'll see."

The parties were all back in place forty-five minutes later and the judge came in promptly at the hour mark. Once everyone sat down he began to speak. "This case, although sad, is an open and shut case. It doesn't matter how long a person has been a member or in leadership.

What counts in a case like this is what's contained in the church bylaws. This morning I did a quick scan of the bylaws and last hour I did a thorough reading. The bylaws of Greenlakes Christian Church specifically give the pastor of the church full authority to select trustees, staff members, and advisors. The pastor also has control of all bank accounts of the church. You trustees may not think it is fair, but I am mandated to rule with the bylaws of the church. These bylaws have not been changed since the church started with the original pastor and his family. Although these policies may have been ignored in the past they still apply. I would suggest that all of you try to work together and blend in the old with the new. It would make no sense for a church split when this situation can be worked out. Judgment for the defendant." With that, Judge Dane slammed the gavel and left the courtroom. The trustees and members were stunned and stormed out of the courtroom. They had been operating the way they pleased for over 15 years since the first pastor passed away and had not thought to take a look at the church bylaws. Pastor Bailey looked at his lawyer. "I knew things would turn out this way, but we needed the judge to tell them that. Because when I found out what the bylaws said, if I had come in and told them that you had full authority they wouldn't have believed me." "Thanks" said Pastor Bailey as he eyed the dejected church members in the hall. "I have some reconciliation to go take care of."

The bottom line: The bylaws are the first and most important item governing the church! Civil courts can't act on the church regarding its affairs. Example, courts can't uphold the Bible if a new pastor says Jesus isn't the only way. They will review the church bylaws and determine who has the authority to make decisions and the court will give those people control of the property. The court says, "we are going to look at the deeds and bylaws and decide who has the right to make decisions and spend the money." In this case the problem arose in when the bylaws said one thing and the old regime had been operating a different way without regard to the bylaws. Although he was not totally sure of it, the pastor was doing everything according to the rules but the new people he put into position thought and operated differently from the old crew and that fact caused the rift. I believe the pastor should have spent time trying to work with the trustees. Nevertheless, the bylaws said he had the authority to make all of the changes that he made. The bylaws are king. GET YOUR BYLAWS IN ORDER NOW!

NEPOTISM IN THE CHURCH

All in the Family

Pastor Charlene Groves was finally able to save enough money to move from having church in her living room to renting a small store front and buying some chairs for her now 60-member congregation to have church. She was a bi-vocational pastor, working 40 hours a week in the auto industry, but she had plenty of time in the evenings and on weekends to properly conduct church business. After a year in the store front she was ready to hire an assistant because now the church was up to 100 members and she could no longer manage it alone and have a full-time job. She was not ready to quit the job, so she knew that she had to get help. Pastor Charlene's heart was right, and she wanted to help those that had stood by her through her journey thus far. However, instead of heeding the voice of the Holy Spirit and hiring Terrance Lake, a relatively new member that just moved into the area and had multiple office and managerial skills, she instead hired her younger sister Brenda. Brenda was coming to the church infrequently. She said she was a Christian, but she was still clubbing and dating men that were unsaved. Pastor Groves thought to herself, "I'll hire Brenda and she will be here with me in the evenings and on Sundays and I will bring her to authentic Christianity, just like I used to train her when we were kids. Brenda had been a secretary to the manager at a leasing company but lost her job when the economy crashed. Since then she had been working part-time clerical jobs and jobs through temp agencies.

Brenda was thrilled to get the job. She had been unemployed for eight months. However, right from the start she asserted herself and let her older sister know that she wasn't going to be in church every Sunday. Instead of putting her foot down right then and making some rules, Pastor Groves smiled and said, "We will see."

Brenda was given the job title "Pastor's Assistant." She was to be a full-time employee working eight hours daily Tuesday through Friday. Brenda was put in charge of answering the phones and taking messages for the pastor, making sure the building was clean and calling a maintenance company if it wasn't, preparing all of the graphics for the church bulletin, managing the new church website and social media platforms, and other duties as they became necessary.

Four months into Brenda's employment the church imploded. Members were bombarding the pastor with complaints not only that Brenda was rude when answering the phone but also that the phone wasn't being answered for hours at a time during the day. One couple was calling in to inform the church that their teenager was in a car accident. When Brenda finally answered the phone hours later she was rude and inconsiderate of their plight. Pastor Groves smoothed it over for her sister by saying that she would get her trained in phone etiquette and recording messages.

In addition, church members had come to Pastor Groves about social media pictures of Brenda with several different men in party settings holding glasses of liquor. One member said that they came up to the church during the week and saw a man leaving the building throwing kisses back at Brenda.

Also, the church website was riddled with typos and had not been updated in the three months since Brenda created it. These allegations had not been addressed by Pastor Groves, as she put off talking to her sister about her behavior as a single Christian woman and as a church employee.

Soon the church was down to forty members and Pastor Groves had the difficult task of telling her sister Brenda that she had to be let go. Brenda had not been publicly disciplined about the allegations because the pastor deemed it a private matter. The pastor's mishandling of these serious issues cost her some of her most loyal members. Moreover, if she had not let her sister go she would have eventually lost the church.

Nepotism is defined as, the practice among those with power or influence of favoring relatives or friends, especially by giving them jobs. This could also include favoritism, preferential treatment, and the old boy (girl) network.

The bottom line: Nepotism has destroyed governments, businesses, and churches for centuries because people of influence continue to select unqualified friends and family members for critical positions over qualified individuals. Don't cause problems in your church by hiring or otherwise favoring family members and friends that are not qualified for the task at hand.

EMBEZZLEMENT IN THE CHURCH

Robbing Peter to Pay Paul

Daisy Lanier was a long-time member of Taylor Road Presbyterian Church. She had worked in the business office since before Pastor Stanford arrived six years ago. Daisy was a retired accountant who first worked part-time then full time for the church. She was a single parent with two grown children and four grandchildren. Daisy was quiet and unassuming. The only thing most members knew about Daisy was that she loved her family.

One year in late February when it was time for the audit, the pastor received a call from their CPA firm stating that Daisy had been putting off the audit for a month. They told the pastor that Daisy at first said she was ill, then said she was on vacation, and her last excuse was that her computer system crashed. The firm wanted to remind the pastor that the bank was looking for the audit by April 30th and they didn't want to be blamed for the delay.

The pastor thought it was strange that Daisy didn't inform him nor the church treasurer that there was a computer crash, and he didn't remember Daisy being sick or taking a vacation in January. After thinking it over and finding no sense in what Daisy had told the auditors, the pastor decided to have the CPA firm come in on the following Saturday to get the audit started because Daisy was going to be out of town the entire week visiting her grandchildren in another state.

The pastor was in for a shock when after working all day Saturday and on Sunday evening the auditors told the pastor that the church deposits were 25% lower than last year. Pastor Stanford knew that giving was up tremendously because the church had a growth spurt after he was interviewed on one of the local television stations about nine months prior to the end of the year.

He asked the auditors to stay through the week and complete the audit with the help of the part-time receptionist and a few loyal retired members. These members were told not to have any communication with Daisy until further notice. At the end of the week it was clear that Daisy had stolen over $54,000 during the course of the previous fiscal year. She had taken the cash funds from various church services. She was able to do this because after the counts for all evening services the funds were locked in her office and she was able to manipulate the count sheet to reflect a lower amount collected in cash. The auditor noted that at first she would just take the funds that were not accompanied by a giving envelope—the funds just tossed into the offering bucket without a paper trail. When she would do that she would change the total for "bucket cash" and adjust the entire count sheet to reflect that lower number. However, towards the end of the fiscal year they noted that she started to take larger sums of cash from the offering envelops of the people that regularly gave in cash.

She would change their total on the count sheets for these night services, then input the correct amount in the computer for their giving statements. So, for example, John Doe really gave $200 and that amount was reflected on his offering envelope. However, Daisy took $140, changed the count sheet to $60 for John Doe's offering, and when she needed to record the offering envelopes for giving statements she would have the correct amount of $200 input into the giving software. She hadn't figured out how to reconcile that system for the auditors to miss her embezzlement during the audit, and that, they think, is why she kept delaying the audit.

When Daisy returned the next Monday, the police were waiting to pick her up and charge her with embezzlement. The auditors had compiled a report on the entire scheme and since she was the only one that handled money in the office, she was the only suspect. Daisy confessed on the spot. In tears she revealed the fact that her newest grandson, born in June of the previous year, had been born with several congenital disabilities and she was taking money to pay for his medical care. She was afraid to ask for help because it was so much money needed, and she didn't think the board of directors would agree to loan her that much.

Embezzlement is defined as theft or misappropriation of funds placed in one's trust or belonging to one's employer.

The bottom line: Have procedures in place to safeguard the church funds from theft. Don't put people in the finance office that are not loyal members, vetted, and qualified. Make sure internal controls are in place to separate duties that may open opportunities for embezzlement. Make sure that more than one person handles the finances and rotate the counters on a regular basis. Watch for changes in staff that would cause them to be financially strapped.

CREDIT AND IDENTITY THEFT IN THE CHURCH

If You Love Me

Rhonda worked in the bookstore at Blackhills AME Church. She was a young, insecure finance major that participated in the young adult's ministry. The finance director thought it would be a good idea to let her work in the bookstore, helping with the sales on Sundays after church. Rhonda was to be trained by the head of the bookstore ministry, Zachary Franklin.

The church bookstore was full of books, videos, and of course the powerful messages that the pastor taught every Sunday and Wednesday. Zachary trained Rhonda and a few other members so that nobody would have to work more than once a week. However, after about two months Rhonda was asking to work in the bookstore every Sunday because she couldn't work on Wednesdays because of her college class load. Zachary agreed and let her work in the bookstore every Sunday after church.

One day the church received a call from a long-time member that her credit card had been hacked and that the only place she has used that particular card in the last two months was in the church bookstore. After that another call came in, and another. It became clear to the finance department at Blackhills that there was a breach in their system and members' credit card information was being compromised.

That night the pastor called an emergency meeting of the board of directors, the finance office staff, and the bookstore staff. Rhonda was not at the meeting because she had a class and didn't get the phone message or the text concerning the meeting. Zachary and the finance team went through several batches of records for the last month and concluded that the breach came from the bookstore and not from the finance office. The finance office did not have credit card information on the offering envelopes because they did not take credit cards as payment. Each member that wanted to use a card was encouraged to go to the church website and select the giving button to give tithes, offerings, and to other ministry categories. However, in the bookstore, the workers had access to the card and the security code when they took the card to swipe or insert it into the card processing machine.

Upon further investigation during the meeting it was noted that the breaches were only on Sunday afternoons, and that Rhonda was the only one that was always working in the bookstore during all of the violations that were called in.

Zachary gave Rhonda a call while they were still in the meeting. She answered her phone, and he asked her to come over to the church immediately. She insisted that she needed to get home from class, but he let her know that it was to her benefit to come into the church office NOW!

Rhonda came in, but she was with a man. Zachary nor the staff had ever seen this man before, and they were not aware that Rhonda was dating. The man was asked to leave and wait outside because this was a private matter. He reluctantly left after he couldn't persuade Rhonda to leave with him. When confronted, Rhonda caved in and told the pastor and members that this man, her boyfriend, said that if she loved him she would take the device he gave her and run the cards through that device when she received them for payment for bookstore items. She admitted that she would take the card then turn around and run it through the hidden device while the members were in conversations and the other bookstore workers were helping other customers.

Rhonda was arrested for credit card theft and so was her boyfriend.

Identity Theft is defined as the fraudulent acquisition and use of a person's private identifying information, usually for financial gain. It is the largest growing form of theft worldwide. Each person has a 1 in 15 chance of having their identity stolen each year, and that number is declining. According to insurance experts, in 2017 identity theft has topped 16 million victims and there are now more social security numbers being stolen than credit card numbers.

The Bottom Line

Do not store any social security numbers or credit card numbers in your church. Do not have credit card numbers on the back of your giving statements for people to turn in for your staff to transact. Set up an online giving portal for people to give online without you having access to their credit card numbers. If you have to retain credit and social security information, as in the case of payroll records, make sure they are locked away and only those in the finance department have access to them.

HARASSMENT AND OTHER SEXUAL ISSUES IN THE CHURCH

The Lord Told Me

Goodwill AME Church welcomed a new member, Fonda Favors. Fonda was a beautiful young lady who had just moved to the city and had been referred to the church by her previous pastor. Pastor Slickness was a married, dynamic, motivational speaker that kept the church members on their feet with his fiery rhyming messages. When Pastor Slickness saw Fonda as she stood up to be greeted as a new member, he gravitated toward her like a magnet. The married pastor started taking more than the usual interest in Fonda. He inquired about her job status and got her a job, and he used his connections in the community to get her moved into a better unit in the same apartment complex into which she had just moved and signed a lease. Moreover, he rushed her through the new members class in two months instead of the usual six months; stating that she had come recommended and had been through the class at her previous church. This treatment was not even a privilege given to ministers that came in from other related churches.

Fonda was very grateful and also attracted to this dynamic pastor. Soon the pastor started a relationship with her saying, "God said for her to service him." Fonda obeyed, and soon entered the underground world of pastor sex partner swapping. Other pastors, married and single, were coming into town bringing women that were not their wives and swapping these women with women the local pastors had, "on the side." At first Fonda was not having sexual relations with anyone but Pastor Slickness. However, six months after this relationship started, the pastor came to Fonda and let her know that a big convention would be held in Florida and that he wanted her to take off work and go to it to represent the church at a booth in the exhibit hall. She agreed and took time off work to go. When she arrived in Florida at the hotel Friday morning, she checked into her room and rested. Pastor Slickness knocked on her door a few hours later. He had with him a fellow pastor from another state. She invited them in and inquired about her duties at the exhibit booth. Pastor Slickness said, "You're not here to work at a booth. I brought you here to entertain Filander here. Pastor Filander was about 20 years older than Fonda, quite portly and quite drunk. Pastor Slickness turned and walked out of the room. Fonda was in shock as this man started to undress. She was wondering what to do, so she immediately grabbed her unpacked bag and slipped down the back stairs, caught a taxi to the airport, paid for a one-way ticket home.

Upon returning home Fonda wrote and mailed a letter of resignation from the church and never returned. She met a nice man at work and she confided in him what had been going on. He was furious and asked her to pursue legal action, but she decided not to because she had initially been complicit in the adulterous relationship with Pastor Slickness.

Sexual Harassment is defined as aggressive pressure or intimidation (typically towards a woman) in a workplace, or other professional or social situation, involving the making of unwanted sexual advances or obscene remarks. There are millions of cases of sexual harassment registered around the country and thousands of those originate in the church! The "Me Too" sexual harassment movement is in full bloom, and sexual harassment in the church is included in this movement as several prominent national pastors have been taken down by allegations of sexual harassment—same sex and opposite sex.

The bottom line: Have clear lines of being able to complain to stop sexual harassment in your church. If people feel like they don't have a voice, your church is more susceptible to lawsuits. It is a safety valve if you have a suggestion box. Do not meet with the opposite sex alone and always have the door open when you meet with members. Do not ride alone with the opposite sex in your car unless they are in the back seat. These measures may save even the appearance of sexual harassment in your church.

RAPE AND MOLESTATION ON CHURCH PROPERTY

Hide and Seek

New Feelings Church of God In Christ was a relatively large church with a huge building. The building, a former elementary school, had been purchased from the local county five years ago and donated to the church by a wealthy member. It was in an ideal location to minister to the poor and nurture at-risk youth. Membership grew fast, as the church was on the bus line and offered job training and other uplift programs.

With this growth came the need for additional security, but the church and the pastor were so busy creating and launching new programs for further growth that security issues fell to the wayside.

One summer day the pastor was approached by one of the deacons. This deacon had noticed that parents had been dropping off their children, ages 8 to 18, at the church for Sunday School, leaving them and not picking them up until church was over. The deacon said that he had seen a massive increase in children in the halls and he was trying to get some help to monitor the increased traffic. That Sunday the pastor made an announcement to the congregation that they were not allowed to drop their children off at church and leave them to go spend the day doing whatever they wanted. He stated that the church was not a daycare center and that if they were to continue to leave their children unattended at the church, any child found without parental supervision would be sent away with the Department of Family and Children Services. The problem with that announcement was that the parents that were leaving their children at the church weren't in church to hear it.

The deacon knew that that announcement wasn't sufficient, but the pastor and the other leaders carried on with their growth and expansion plans. Three weeks later the police showed up at the church after the Sunday service while the leaders and staff were winding up for the day. The pastor was informed that a woman had brought her 14-year-old daughter into the local hospital because the girl claimed she had been raped that morning in one of the classrooms at the church. The police report stated that the girl, who had been dropped off for "youth service" that morning, was crying when she was picked up after church. The girl stated that a boy around 16-years-old told her to come into one of the classrooms after Sunday school so that he could show her the beautiful tropical fish that the teacher had placed in the room. Not noticing that the boy was only telling her about the fish she went in. Yes, there were fish in the room and after she took a minute to admire all of the colorful tiny creatures she headed to the door. She had not noticed that the boy had locked the door and at that time he raped her.

The church was sued for negligence and the young man, whose mother had also dropped him off at 8:00 A.M. and left to go shopping for the day, was bound over to the juvenile court once he was identified.

Rape is a type of sexual assault usually involving sexual intercourse or other forms of sexual penetration perpetrated against a person without that person's consent. Statutory Rape is sexual intercourse by an adult with a person below a statutorily designated age (a minor).

The bottom line: It's all about Procedure. Don't leave doors open or unlocked while people are in the building, especially if you have a large building. Have deacons check the rooms daily and during every service. Have good security cameras all over the church and someone that regularly monitors them if your church is large. If you know someone in the church has been in trouble from a sexual standpoint (a predator) keep an eye on them and even follow them to the bathroom when they leave during service. If there are allegations of rape handle them immediately, obtaining all of the facts and, if necessary, contacting the local authorities.

Under no circumstances should a Sunday school teacher, counselor or church worker take a child or children and drive them anywhere without other adults being present. Field trips should require at least two trusted adults.

IMPROPER COUNSELING IN THE CHURCH

Is it the Money or the Safety?

Paul and Stephanie Jones were a married couple in crisis. Paul had a drug problem that he hid from Stephanie while they were dating, and she had just found out about it a year ago. They attended First Saint Shelby Catholic Church and had been members for two years. During the eight years of their marriage the couple had two boys and the boys were great students in school.

Stephanie had had enough when Paul's drug problem started to escalate. Paul came home one day and hit her because she didn't keep the food warm for him. He was due to come home around 7:00 P.M. but didn't arrive until after midnight. Stephanie had gone to bed and Paul, angry and high on drugs, slapped her for not waiting up and not having his food ready. Stephanie called the church to set up a counseling session.

Initially Paul said that he would never attend counseling but when Stephane threatened to leave and take the boys, Paul agreed to go. There were a few joint sessions and then it was determined by the assigned counselors that Paul needed extensive individual counseling. During the counseling sessions it was clear that Paul needed additional outside assistance due to his drug problems. A rehabilitation center was recommended for Paul, and he went to the center on a Saturday to get some information.

After interviewing with the rehabilitation center the center recommended that to get Paul healed and back on track to a healthy life, he needed to be formally admitted for treatment for at least six months. Paul was not sure this would work because Stephanie didn't make enough money to take care of the bills alone for six months and they had no savings. Besides that, his job would then know that he had a drug problem and he could be fired.

Paul, at Stephanie's request, decided to make an appointment with the Bishop to find out if the church could help out with the household finances for the six months that he was to be in rehabilitation. They wanted to find out this information before Paul said anything to his company. During the meeting, Paul even suggested that if the church could pay the bills that Stephanie couldn't handle during that time, he would gladly pay the church back when he was released and back to work.

The Bishop told Paul that he needed to keep his job and not go to a rehab center, and not let his job know that he was being counseled for drug issues because he may lose his job. He told Paul that the important thing was to make sure the household finances were intact, and bills paid; and that the church was not willing or able to help the couple.

The Bishop told Paul about a special healing ritual that he should register for, and that if he went through this process he would be healed of the desire to take drugs.

Paul attended the special ritual that was held a year later, and he sporadically attended counseling sessions, but the real help was not coming because of the substance abuse and what it was doing to his mind.

Five years later Stephanie took the boys and left Paul after he had given up on being healed. He had lost his job because they found out via his coming to work high. When Stephanie left she immediately filed for a restraining order because Paul had become even more violent. Within two weeks of her leaving, Paul went to Stephanie's job and shot her dead in the parking lot as she got out of the car to enter the building. He was arrested and imprisoned, and the boys, who were now both teenagers, went to live with an uncle.

This uncle, Stephanie's younger brother, sued the church and the Bishop and received a settlement that would take care of the boys all the way through adulthood. The uncle won the case based on lousy counsel given to Paul by the Bishop. The Bishop was held responsible because he told Paul to avoid the life-saving help of the very successful rehabilitation center that Paul had visited.

Counsel is defined as advice, especially advice that is given formally. There are several excellent church counseling licensing programs around the country that will train church counselors concerning what is and is not appropriate counsel for members. These programs have been approved by special boards and licensing authorities and they ensure that ongoing training is available for counselors on staff at churches. Everyone in the church that is a leader or minister is not automatically in the position to be a counselor and because many churches rely on their untrained ministers to council members they are leaving themselves open to lawsuits.

The bottom line: Have training in the church and send the lay counselors to special Christian counseling schools. Proper training would have directed the Bishop in how to avoid this sad partially true story. Counselors need to be well trained. If they don't know how to counsel they could ruin a marriage or even get someone killed.

IGNORING PRIVACY RIGHTS IN THE CHURCH

It is crucial for the leaders of a church or ministry to know when it is legal to circulate private information. Even an ingenuous letter may subject the sender to liability for invasion of privacy. Case in point, Duncan v. Paterson and the Moody Church.

Duncan v. Paterson and the Moody Church

Facts:

Erwin Lutzer, senior pastor of The Moody Church in Chicago, was accused of sending letters to leaders of the Hope Church regarding the alleged behavior of its pastor, Richard Duncan. The letters contained information provided to the Moody Church by people who knew Duncan. The letters stated that Duncan had an improper relationship with a woman who was not his wife, that he had filed for divorce, that he abused alcohol, that he mishandled personal funds, and that he used duplicitous means to access the bank accounts of the Hope Church. Duncan testified that once these letters were sent by Lutzer, the membership of the Hope Church drastically decreased, the church could no longer pay Duncan to be senior pastor, and Duncan was not able to find another job.

Before becoming senior pastor of the Hope Church, Duncan was an assistant pastor at the Moody Church, which had licensed and ordained Duncan as a minister. The letters Lutzer sent to the Hope Church detailed the Moody Church's decision to rescind Duncan's licensing and ordination as a result the behavior mentioned within. Therefore, Lutzer argued to the Court that his sending of the letters was protected by the ecclesiastical abstention doctrine, which says that civil courts may not decide the accuracy of interpretations of religious text or decisions relating to the governance of a religious organization. The Appellate Court found the ecclesiastical abstention doctrine was not applicable in this case. The Court explained that by sending the letters to persons outside the Moody Church, Lutzer's action was unrelated to the governance of the Moody Church. This decision was despite the fact that the letters related to the Moody Church's actions in rescinding Duncan's licensing and ordination. The Appellate Court also found that distributing these letters in no way related to the interpretation of religious text even though the statements in the letters describing Duncan's behavior were followed by references to supporting text from the Bible.

Court Decision:
In a jury trial the jury found Lutzer liable to Duncan for "false light invasion of privacy" for distributing the letters and ordered a monetary judgment against him in the amount of $276,306. Lutzer appealed.

The Appellate Court mentioned that the letters contained at least one false statement and that some of the statements in the letters were included without any fact-finding. The court posited that even if Lutzer had no knowledge that any of the letter's statements were false, the jury could have still properly found Lutzer made the allegations with careless disregard for their falseness. Therefore, the Illinois Appellate Court for the Second District affirmed the jury verdict against Lutzer.

OTHER CHURCH RELATED COURT CASES AND WHY IT IS CRITICAL THAT YOU UNDERSTAND THEM

I have done research to try and help churches prevent lawsuits. Now more than ever the Church needs to protect herself from predators without and within the four walls. I have selected these additional court cases to share with you because they will be of great help in making pastors, church leaders, and administrators understand how vital it is to be legally prepared for just about anything. Because just about anything can happen when you have a church, and especially when you are preaching and teaching the uncompromised word of God. Understand that the devil is already angry about the fact that you exist. When you start to grow and thrive then the battle is on—spiritually, mentally, physically, financially, socially, and legally. Understanding the premise behind these cases will help you prepare for many of the obstacles that Satan throws at you and your church.

These cases involve civil law issues, such as the ones that I discussed above, and cases about who has the legal authority to decide a case when a church body is involved. I know people absolutely loathe reading court cases, as do I. But I will give you the thumbnail version by describing the facts that surround the case, and the court's decisions. Here we go!

WATSON V. JONES, 80 U.S. (13 Wall.) 679 (1871), is a United States Supreme Court case.

This case is the bedrock of all ecclesiastical law. Although it's over 100 years old, this is still good case law. Watson v. Jones defined the types of churches and the characteristics of each type. It also lays out many principals that still exist today.

Facts:
The case was based upon a dispute regarding the Third or Walnut Street Presbyterian Church in Louisville, Kentucky. Two opposing factions were claiming control of the church building and other property.

Court Decision:
The Court held that in cases about church property disputes,

1. Courts cannot rule on the truth or falsity of a religious teaching.
2. Where a previous authority structure existed before the dispute, courts should defer to the decision of that structure, and
3. In the absence of such an internal authority structure, courts should defer to the wishes of a majority of the congregation.

Because the Walnut Street Presbyterian Church had a distinct internal governing structure, the court gave control of the property to that assembly, even though it was only backed by a minority of the congregation.

The Court believed that their opinion issued a spirit of freedom for religious groups, and independence from secular control or manipulation. The decision ensured that churches had the power to decide for themselves, free from state interference, matters of church governance as well as those of faith and doctrine.

The power of civil courts to rule in church property disputes was drastically limited, the Court held, because to allow resolution of doctrinal disputes in court was to endanger First Amendment values. What a court must do, it was held, is to review the church rules, and if the church is hierarchical and tasks determination of ecclesiastical issues in a specific body, the declaration by that body is determinative, while if the church is congregational and prescribes action by a majority vote, that decision will prevail.

MCCLURE v. SALVATION ARMY (Information about this case was gleaned from the Pew Research Center—http://www.pewforum.org/2011/03/31/churches-in-court3/)

Facts:
This case was about what's called the "ministerial exception." It arose out of a statutory exemption from one specific employment regulation, Title VII of the Civil Rights Act of 1964, which bans employers from discriminating against their employees based on race, color, religion, sex, or national origin. Title VII contains language giving religious institutions the ability to provide employment preference to members of their own faith when hiring any type of worker, whether or not that worker performs religious duties. But Title VII does not expressly let religious organizations discriminate on the basis of other protected

characteristics, such as race or gender. This omission left unanswered a difficult question: When hiring clergy and other employees who perform primarily religious functions, could religious organizations discriminate not just on the basis of religion but also on the basis of other protected characteristics such as race or gender?

The case involved a woman, Billie B. McClure, who had been a Salvation Army officer, the Salvation Army's equivalent of an ordained minister. After she complained that male officers were receiving higher salaries and better benefits than female officers, the Salvation Army fired McClure. She then sued the Salvation Army on the grounds that her firing constituted gender discrimination, in violation of Title VII. After a federal trial court ruled for the Salvation Army, McClure appealed to the 5th U.S. Circuit Court of Appeals.

The Salvation Army made two arguments to the appeals court in defense of its decision to fire McClure: (1) that the exemption for religious employers in Title VII allowed them to engage in gender discrimination with respect to the employment of clergy; and (2) that even if the exemption did not allow gender discrimination in such a case, the statutory prohibition on gender discrimination still did not apply to the Salvation Army in this instance because the First Amendment guarantees religious organizations the right to make ministerial employment decisions free from government regulation.

Court Decision:

The 5th Circuit rejected the Salvation Army's first claim —that the Title VII exemption for religious employers allowed it to engage in gender discrimination. The court explained that the exemption relieves religious employers from liability only when they discriminate on the basis of the employee's religion. Therefore, the court said, when a religious organization discriminates against an employee on the basis of Title VII's other protected characteristics—race, color, sex, and national origin—the law's exemption does not protect the organization from liability.

After rejecting this argument, the 5th Circuit turned its attention to the Salvation Army's second claim—namely that the Free Exercise Clause mandates that religious organizations be free from government regulation when making employment decisions concerning their religious leaders. In considering this argument, the court cited a series of Supreme Court decisions, stretching back to *Watson v. Jones,* holding that the First Amendment prohibits the government from regulating "matters of church government and administration." Based on these Supreme Court decisions, the 5th Circuit reasoned that traditional anti-discrimination protections, including those contained in Title VII, do not apply to a religious organization's ministerial employment decisions. Therefore, the court concluded, because McClure was the Salvation Army's functional equivalent of an ordained minister, the Salvation Army had the constitutional right to fire her, in spite of the general prohibition on gender discrimination in employment contained in Title VII.

The doctrine announced in *McClure* soon became known as the "ministerial exception." In the almost 40 years since the *McClure* ruling, nearly all of the nation's federal appeals courts have embraced this exception, and no federal appeals court has ever rejected it.

TAMARA CLAIBORNE, AND NOEL HAVERHABIB V. WATER OF LIFE COMMUNITY CHURCH

A recent church litigation survey conducted by ***Church Law & Tax Report*** discloses that securities law violations represent the second highest source of damages in civil litigation involving churches.

The following case involves the church leadership bringing in someone to teach and then offer investments that turned out to be illegitimate. The plaintiffs are not suing the individuals responsible for their financial loss, they are suing the church that brought in the guilty parties. Why? It's called the deep pocket theory. The deep pocket theory reveals that when someone is injured and seeks financial restitution they will research and find and then sue the person or entity in the chain of events that has the most money. When someone at the church violates another person and there is a credible legal issue the person harmed will usually go after the church even if they don't sue the violator. That's because usually the violator has no money and it would be a waste of time to sue that person or even include him/her in the lawsuit. This is the main reason that the church needs to be extra careful about how it treats financial teaching on church grounds, and whom it brings in to conduct financial education. Here's the case.

Facts:
Two former members of the Water of Life Community Church filed a federal class action lawsuit against the church on April 21, 2017, claiming negligence, unfair business practices, and violations of California consumer law.

The former members claim that the scheme involved an elder of the church named Paul Ricky Mata. The lawsuit says that Mata is a convicted swindler and that the church had him on staff teaching members investment strategies.

According to the injured parties, Mata has been at Water of Live since it was founded in 1990, and is a close friend of Dan Carroll, the church CEO. ***(Note that neither Mata nor Carroll are parties to the lawsuit)***

The plaintiffs say that Mata, an elder and teacher, was tasked to teach members of their school of ministry how to invest and manage their finances. They say that members were strongly influenced to complete a series of financial courses because the church required its members to take part in them so they could move up in rank and be listed in the church directory.

Records show that his securities licenses expired in 2012. According to the lawsuit, "Mata had a host of unregistered securities and illegal investment advisory arrangements" he pushed off on trusting church members, promising "indestructible wealth" through various classes the church mandated members to complete.

According to the complaint, several church members raised questions about the efficacy of Mata's financial curriculum, but the church dismissed their calls for a more credentialed personal financial adviser.

The members say Mata's deception ended in 2015, when the Securities & Exchange Commission filed an emergency action against Mata and divulged he had swindled hundreds of people out of $14.5 million. The two members say they lost the $1.24 million in their transactions with Mata, and that CEO Carroll rebuked them when they went to him for financial help.

The former members note in the lawsuit that Water of Life is one of the richest and fastest growing **businesses** in the area, and that it is currently building a $20 million complex. They are seeking class certification and actual, compensatory and statutory damages.

As of this writing this case is still in the court system.

Here's the bottom line when it comes down to financial dealings with the membership.

Make sure that when you have financial teaching:

1. The teacher has financial credentials and has shown proof.
2. The teacher is teaching exactly what you want them to cover.
3. The teacher is sharing Biblical and business financial truths.
4. The teacher is NOT offering any investments on church grounds!

Conclusion

Here's my two cents when it comes to saving the church from lawsuits:

> Develop clear and concise bylaws and review them regularly. Write policies. Succession policies. Have clear rules. If it says this is the group that needs to determine how much is spent for building improvement, then do it that way.
>
> If there is a problem make sure a procedure is written out to solve it. Stay away from letting investment opportunities into the church.

PILLAR FIVE

PREPARING FOR PERPETUITY

According to Investopedia, the financial definition of perpetuity is, "a constant stream of identical cash flows with no end."

I entitled this Pillar, "Preparing For Perpetuity" because the church needs to be as wise as serpents when it comes down to making sure there are funds always available for ministry. Most of the time the funds that come into the ministry come from the membership. Thus, if the membership is broke the church is usually broke. However, if the membership can be taught to be financially literate and if they learn the secrets of the wealthy then the church will have perpetual funds to do the work of the Lord.

Many pastors and congregants have been programmed with the wrong mindset about wealth. Many say that Jesus was poor, and that Christians should take a vow of poverty because money is evil. They don't mention the fact that several wealthy people funded Jesus' ministry. In fact, today many of the largest, most effective ministries in the world are funded by millionaire and multi-millionaire Christians.

The Bible actually says, in 1 Timothy 6:10, "The love of money is a root of all **kinds** of evil". There is no mention of money being evil in and of itself. So, should Christians be poor and broke, or should we live in opulence? There is an answer to this question and we will discuss it before we discuss wealth creation.

WHAT DOES THE BIBLE SAY ABOUT WEALTH?

God's people, the nation of Israel, have been blessed with riches from the beginning. In Genesis God showed that He blessed His people with gold, which He said was good (Genesis 2:11–12).

Because Genesis set a precedent for gold being good (the law of first mention) we can conclude based on the several mentions of gold in Genesis that it was used as provision for God's people. Father Abraham, (Abram in Genesis) was "very rich in livestock, in silver, and in gold" (Genesis 13:2). So, if Abraham was rich why would Christians conclude that being rich is evil?

In addition to God blessing His people with wealth (using gold as the primary example) the Scripture that says the wealth of the sinner is stored up for the righteous (Proverbs 13:22) is played out in Genesis 41:42, "Then Pharaoh took his signet ring off his hand and put it on Joseph's hand;

and he clothed him in garments of fine linen **and put a gold chain around his neck."**

I believe that Christians are supposed to be wealthy. However, the problem with Christians being wealthy these days is that many are laying up that wealth for themselves and not for the furtherance of the gospel. Over the centuries as Christianity developed a bad reputation a part of that blight has been the use of church funds to create a lavish lifestyle for the church leaders.

If we do as the Christians of old and fund ministry with our resources, then I believe that God will continually bless us to have enough to fund ministry and live a spiritually and financially rich life. My belief comes from the discussion between Jesus and the disciples in the parable of the rich young ruler. In Luke 18:18–30 Jesus mentions how hard it is to get into heaven and the disciples were disturbed. Then He said, "Assuredly, I say to you, there is no one who has left house or parents or brothers or wife or children, for the sake of the kingdom of God, who shall not receive many times more in this present time, and in the age to come eternal life" (Luke 18:29–30). "In this present time" precludes Christians from always being impoverished, as I see it, so we need to start building wealth for Kingdom Advancement—seeking Him first, and all the other things will follow (Matthew 6:33). That's the end of my Bible study for the day. Now let's talk about building Kingdom wealth the right way.

HOW CAN THE CHURCH GET OUT OF DEBT?

One of the largest problems that I see is that the Church is drowning in the same pool of debt as the world. Either Christians were not taught proper money management, or they choose to ignore it and partake in the earn-spend cycle with the world. Let me define the earn-spend cycle.

Earn-Spend Cycle:
You get paid on Friday, go to the Mall after work and buy Coach and Gucci, go to the club Friday night and Saturday night, throw $25 in the bucket at church in between dozing off, pay your rent and Benz note and Monday morning you are Broke! Two weeks later you do it all over again. Too many Christians are in this sad predicament. How can we help the unsaved if we are sinking in the debt pool along with them?

Let's talk a little about debt. There are different schools of thought concerning the definition of debt. One school says anything you owe is a debt and you should owe no man, which has become all but impossible today, unless you are a Gates or a Rockefeller. The more modern school of thought concerning debt says that when you borrow or use credit cards and can't pay the bills when they're due, you are in debt.

In ancient times, if you owed someone and couldn't repay him or her, that creditor had the right to put you in prison until you repaid every dime. The creditor would then own everything that belonged to you, including your spouse, children, and all of your possessions!

Today, I think debt encompasses more than either of these definitions. Debt is the result of a mindset—a mentality that we must destroy.

Let's start off by talking about the mindset of the poor. The poor buy liabilities, and their minds are focused on survival. The mindset of the poor is, "I can't change my circumstances—I need to make the best of what I have."

Many of these people are not looking for a way out or a way up. They just want to survive. Constantly in a situation where their expenses are more than their income, many take to illegal means to support their families or their habits. I call this a poverty mentality. Do you know any of your church members that have a poverty mentality? Don't think that everyone that's in this category is a heathen not attending church!

Many poor people settle for being poor because changing their circumstances requires energy and thought that they are not willing to expend and employ. Tragically, this mentality is becoming more widespread in our society as we see welfare rolls and crime rates increase. I believe the church that gets involved with work and entrepreneurship programs will stifle this downward spiral into hopelessness and can actually bring people to Christ.

There are some people who are not mentally or physically able to change their circumstances, but the vast majority of poor people in the United States can change their lives with just a few important adjustments. I have seen it happen and know that it is possible.

Lydia grew up in the projects with two younger brothers. Her mother was a single parent but instead of acting like a victim Lydia's mother worked two jobs to make ends meet. She also taught her children a good work ethic and did not ever let them use their poverty as an excuse to gain pity or unearned rewards. As a result, Lydia worked hard and put herself through college with few student loans. Today, Lydia is an executive at a large multinational corporation; she travels around the world for this company and is enjoying life, having escaped the poverty cycle from which she came.

Now let's talk about the middle-class. Middle-class people buy liabilities, often believing that they are assets. Society has placed a picture of the American dream in front of the middle-class and they are chasing that picture like a donkey chases a carrot. They work harder and longer to keep up, but their fundamental situation doesn't change. They get caught in the earn/spend cycle, are very frustrated, and sometimes give up on their dreams.

These are the people with "decent" corporate or blue-collar jobs. They go out and buy big houses and cars and have credit card and other consumer debt that is constantly drowning them. Most people in churches are in this category.

These are the people who get paid on Friday and immediately go to the mall to buy the latest and greatest gadgets and name-brand clothes. By Monday they are "broke, busted, and disgusted," and they survive until the next paycheck, when they do it all over again. Some are not even aware that they are literally two paychecks away from living on the street. Daily, I drive in my neighborhood and others around town, and I never fail to see furniture and clothes on front lawns, as people have been evicted or their homes have been foreclosed. Most of the churches with which I have a relationship are full of middle-classed people that are not tithing because they are caught in the earn-spend cycle. Do your members live in the earn-spend cycle?

As a result of this middle-class mindset:
Over 40% of all American families are in debt at a given time. Credit card debt averages around $16,000 per household and total consumer debt averages around $32,000 per household. Some people are actually borrowing money from one credit card to pay the minimum balance due on another one.

How did all of this get started in the first place? Did people always amass a lot of debt? Here are some answers.

In the early 1920s debt was uncommon. In fact, Americans usually only borrowed to buy homes. Back then, loans were for seven years or less, based on the Bible. Deuteronomy says, "At the end of every seven years you shall grant a remission of debts" (15:1). This was a time when the Bible was still sacred in the minds of main street America.

When thousands of GI's returned after World War II, the trend of consumer debt started. Americans had lots of disposable income and were well able to handle debt.

As the debt craze escalated, by the mid-1960s, Americans could buy almost anything on credit. Major retailers became lenders; some even charged higher interest rates than banks! This was possible because the salesperson had the customer right there as a captive audience, and after the big sales pitch, the customer just signed on the dotted line without thinking about the higher interest charges.

During the late 1960s, women started to enter the workforce and the lenders were forced to start including both incomes when considering a home loan. Thus, housing prices skyrocketed because sellers knew that two-income couples could "afford" to pay more for homes. This tactic is typical of the greedy banking society in which we live.

The results were as follows: by 2002 the median income per family was $49,000. Based on that income, an average home should have cost $98,000, but was selling for just under $108,000. Now housing costs are off the charts as the real estate craze ramps back up after the 2008 stock market crash.

By the early 1970s, due to the profit seen by big retail stores like Sears and Montgomery Ward, the credit card binge was in full bloom. Some retailers made as much on financing as they made on merchandise!

These days' banks and retailers make much more with the interest and late fees than the costs of the items purchased.

The difference between the early 1970s and now is that Americans were more hard-working, ethical, and debt-conscious then. There was much more trust that the loans would be paid on time and eventually paid off. Today, people file for bankruptcy at the drop of a hat, so lenders don't mind sticking it to everyone with outrageously high interest rates.

The problem with all of this debt is that the national debt is also increasing due to the government borrowing more and more from the Federal Reserve (which is not "federal", has no reserves, and has never been audited) and printing more and more paper money based on government whims, not tangible goods.

When there is not enough income earned to cover credit card debt and interest, the average consumer will now go bankrupt, but the government will just go out and borrow more from the "Fed."

This is an escalating cycle of debt and soon the house of cards is bound to fall. According to a financial news article, Americans spend over $22.9 billion on clothes, $3.2 billion on electronics, and $11.6 billion on furniture put into homes that in many cases are rented. In addition, we spend $46.7 billion on new cars. Americans and others are not paying attention to the coming economic tsunami, and these are the people who will be hit the hardest if the principles in this book are ignored.

So how do we escape this cycle of debt? In my book, *How to Escape the Rat Race: Four Keys to Acquire the Life of Your Dreams* I explain how we can get out of personal debt, but how do we get the church out of debt? Because I believe the easiest way to get out of debt is to increase income while decreasing expenses both these topics will be discussed in detail in this pillar. First, we will talk about decreasing church expenses.

DECREASING CHURCH EXPENSES

Eliminating Some Ministries and/or Auxiliaries

It's always hard to tell a parishioner that the ministry they head up needs to be dissolved. Sometimes this act will cause loss of members. However, when a church has a ministry/auxiliary that is using a lot of the church resources but not bringing in members or money, then it's time to re-evaluate and maybe dismantle it.

For example, every year Dave at First Mount Pinnacle Baptist hosted a 5K race against drug abuse. Dave, a former all-star athlete and a former drug addict, loves to run and tell his story of transformation. At first, Pastor Wiggins thought it was a great idea. The first year many of the church members and some of the neighbors participated. But now, in its 5th year, there are just a handful of participants, and this has been the case for the last two years.

The way Dave has the event coordinated it costs the church $3,800 because streets have to be blocked off, medics have to be hired in case of medical emergencies and everyone that completes the race receives a trophy. Now that there is only a handful of people participating, Pastor Wiggins had to tell Dave that the expense is too great for the church to continue to carry the event. Pastor Wiggins told Dave that he has the full support of the church if he wants to continue with the race, but he would have to pay the $3,800 out of his own pocket.

In this case Dave could either have his feelings hurt and leave the church or find a way to keep it going and have greater participation.

As an aside, the best way to have good ministries in the church and not hurt feelings is to follow a plan I heard from a popular northwestern ministry. If a member brings a ministry idea to the elders it first has to be in writing along with the budget. The elders will evaluate whether the ministry idea is in line with the mission and vision of the ministry. If they decide that the ministry will benefit the church and the Body of Christ, they inform the member, in writing that he or she can start the ministry. The only requisite is that the member has to fund this new ministry for one year, and if the ministry is successful the church will take over and fund it from then on.

My children are grown now, and when we go out to dinner they always ask me who's paying. If I say I'm paying they will get meals that cost $30 plus. If I say everyone is paying for their own meal they will spend around $12. It's the same mentality that you will find in many churches. Lots of times members think the church has unlimited funds and they will devise projects to spend the church money without a clear understanding of the whole financial picture. With the "you fund it for a year" concept everyone will find out if this member got the ministry idea from God and is willing to put their ALL into it. It's very easy to waste other people's money when you don't have "skin in the game." Using this strategy is just being good stewards of God's money.

Negotiating a Lower Interest Rate on Mortgages and Other Debt

There are many financial gurus out there and the one thing I agree with them on is the fact that everyone, including the church, should go and negotiate a lower interest rate on any debt that has been acquired. Many times, the church mortgage is large and that makes the church one of the smaller banks largest customers and one of the larger banks most valuable customers. If the pastor and financial officer go into the bank and show that they are consistent with payments, it's possible that the bank will agree to lower the interest rate. A lower rate can mean saving $500 or more per month in interest for many church mortgages.

Monitoring Utility Bills

When I review church books one of the largest expenses that I see, after the mortgage, is the energy (electric and gas) bill. When a church is medium to large it is usually still much larger than the average home, thus the cost to keep the temperature comfortable can be budget breaking. In addition. The water bills can be high if members don't make sure they turn off the water at the sink, or if they don't let the maintenance staff know when there is a "running toilet."

Some of the things a church can do to keep utility costs low are:

- Keep the temperature steady in summer and winter.
- Turn the heat down or air conditioning up when the building is empty.

- Keep shades over doors and windows in summer that would let in lots of sun.
- Fix gaps in doors so that cold and heat won't escape.
- Check into solar panels.
- Keep lights off in rooms that aren't being used.
- Put timers on lights like the bathroom lights and classroom lights.
- Check faucets at the end of each day to ensure that they are turned off.
- Check for faulty plumbing and leaky toilets.

Being Strategic about Gifts and Benevolence

Most churches don't have a benevolence ministry or some system when it comes to giving gifts and caring for members in their time of grief. When looking at church finances I see that a significant amount of money goes to giving gifts and to helping the bereaved. Here are some ideas about keeping gift giving and benevolence costs down:

- Limit the number of churches to which you give gifts. I've seen small churches send larger churches, with which they have no relationship, invitations to their anniversary so they can bring an anniversary gift.
- Set a policy about which deceased relatives qualify your members to receive flowers. For example, only send flowers if it's the member's parent, sibling spouse or child. Send a sympathy card to the member to express your sorrow for any other relatives. Second cousin Bessie May Taylor that was 99 years old doesn't get flowers from the church.

- Put a very caring but firm policy in place for members asking for benevolence. Make sure that policy includes a completed form which includes their family dynamics, and a limit to the amount they can receive and the number of times they can receive help. Also, make sure that financial counseling is included.

Once a church asked me to do some financial counseling for a woman that was repeatedly coming to ask for help with her bills. She was a single parent and was claiming that the child's father was not paying child support. By the time I was brought into the picture she had already asked for financial help twice.

I asked her to bring in all of her bills and income so that we could devise a budget. She reluctantly did it because the church told her that she couldn't get any more money if she didn't comply. This woman was spending more than what she made on her job and supplementing her lifestyle with credit cards.

Once I reviewed her income and expenses I made recommendations, like cutting down on the beauty shop and nail shop visits, dropping the gym membership and walking around the park instead, and getting rid of the cable TV. I gave her a budget that excluded these items and would have her paying all of her bills on time, including the credit cards, with a little left over to save for herself and her child.

She was very grateful for the information, or so I thought. She ended up leaving the church shortly after the consultation because she was "on the hunt" for a man, and the hair, nails, and gym membership were a large part of her plan. The cable television kept her child occupied while she did the things she wanted to do, like talk on the phone and entertain guests.

You have to realize that people will spend their money on what they want and come to you personally and to the church for what they need. It happens to many of us regularly. That's why I take the advice of my Italian mentor, "Don't tell nobody nuttin'." I try to keep my personal finances to myself for the most part because when people think you have money they are not ashamed to ask for some of it. Back in the early 2000s I had a "stash" of money, $16,000 to be exact, that I put aside as a sort of slush fund. I was excited about my growing business and shared it with my friends and family, thinking that they would rejoice with me. After the rejoicing was over people started asking for money for things like mortgages, rent, and even investments. I helped some of them out by loaning them funds, and never got any of that money back. The church is not a bank. Make sure everyone knows that.

When the Finances Get Funny

Churches will have the occasional decrease in income for summer and holidays. But when your downturn lasts longer than expected, it's time to find creative ways to decrease the church's expenses in order to remain viable. In addition to the ones mentioned above, here are some areas that can be adjusted so that the church won't fall into severe debt:

- Have volunteers do landscaping instead of paying a company.

- Replace other contracted services with church volunteers (pest control).
- Get rid of monthly expenses like water and coffee delivery services.
- Close the vents off rooms that are not being used.
- Limit use of the church vehicles to church service pick up and drop off.
- Reduce or eliminate spending on conferences and special events.
- Shut down the church several days a week and have staff work from home.
- Stop printing bulletins for a while and send all announcements via e-mail and social media.
- Limit charges to the church credit card(s).
- Postpone some repairs and maintenance until more funds are available.
- Cut down on the purchase and use of supplies.

INCREASING CHURCH INCOME

In order for us to improve our finances, things can't stay as they are. The definition of insanity is to do the same things over and over and expecting different results. We have been operating in insanity by going through the same weekly rituals all the way up to the Sunday offering with the same results.

On the personal side, church folks have been keeping the same spending habits, and putting money in the same failing investments that the professional gurus have been telling us about for the last five decades. It's time to get out of the insanity mindset and our circle of sameness and improve our finances and the finances of the church!

It's interesting to me that foreigners come to this country, whether legally or not, and before you know it they have a store or some type of business up and running. They hire only their relatives, who then start their own businesses. They seem to grasp the fact that in order to make it in this country, they have to stick together and improve their finances, which usually start out at zero or sometimes less. Although some come here with savings from their home country, most come with just a little money in their pockets and some even come in debt, having to pay someone for their transportation to the States. I really wish the church would think and act the same way as these people do.

The only way for the church and the congregants to really improve our finances is to **reduce our expenses and/or increase our income.** We have discussed decreasing our expenses. Now we will discuss increasing our income for maximum financial empowerment and Kingdom Advancement. This section is geared toward those of you that are very serious and want to be on the fast track to financial freedom, personally, for your church and for the entire Body of Christ.

The entire concept here is that if the church members learn to build wealth and they are faithful Christians then the church will begin to get out of debt and become a place with funds for kingdom building. So, I am first concentrating on individual wealth building. Once those that take heed start to tithe and give offerings from their gains, the church will prosper.

IMPROVING YOUR NET WORTH

Most people think that assets are things you own or buy, like homes and cars. However, we know that assets are things that put money into your pocket.

Examples of real assets are:

- Profitable rental property
- A profitable business
- Income investments
- Savings
- Precious metals
- Agricultural land

Most people think that liabilities consist of what you owe on the things that you buy; we know that liabilities are a lot more than that. Our homes are liabilities unless they bring money to our pockets, as in the case of rental property.

People have challenged me and said that their homes are assets without being rental property. The question that I ask is, "How is the home bringing money into your pocket?" It still needs painting, roofing and other maintenance on a regular basis, and if you skip paying the property taxes to the county for a while, you will see who really owns this so-called asset."

Other liabilities are cars, vacations, furniture, and credit cards. Some people say that our children are also liabilities, but I don't want to say that and spark the heated debate that always occurs when that statement is made in a public forum.

Conventional wisdom says that your net worth is assets minus liabilities. Banks and other financial institutions would like you to have a high net worth or low debt to asset ratio if you are applying for a loan of any type.

It's very hard and sometimes impossible to get a loan when you have low or negative net worth. But interestingly enough, once you achieve a high net worth, you may not even have to worry about getting bank loans because your assets should pay for your liabilities. Many wealthy people are in this position and are able to pay cash for cars or boats; some are even able to pay cash for homes.

Our goal is to have a high net worth and start investing for our futures, so we must get out of debt, get out of debt, get out of debt!

About Increasing Income

All financial advisors will tell you not to spend more money than you earn. When we hear that slogan we always think we have to cut back, delay purchases, skimp, and penny pinch.

My philosophy about not spending more than I earn is to just increase the amount I earn! I focus on creating more value and revenue in my life rather than having a poverty outlook. The key is to make money faster than I spend money. That takes a lot of forethought and creativity.

I see so many people being penny wise and pound foolish in their lives, thinking that they're building wealth. They throw the baby out with the bathwater by not being increase conscious. Increase consciousness is your ability to focus on ways to increase your income, thus building wealth, even if these ways cause you to spend a little more than you normally spend.

For me, being wise about spending entails growing my businesses, not just reducing my expenses. For example, when I conduct seminars I chose to use high-end hotels. I used to use my basement to save money. My basement is large, clean, set up like a classroom and has tables and a small refrigerator to accommodate snacks and drinks that cost an arm and a leg at a hotel. However, I stopped doing the seminars in the basement because while I was saving money I didn't realize that I was damaging my status as a wealth creation specialist. People would see me as a saver, someone with lots of financial knowledge making wise spending decisions, but not a wealth creator.

My guests couldn't see past the fact that I live in a lower-middle-class neighborhood even though my home is large and immaculate. I didn't realize that in order to grow my business and reputation as a financial expert and wealth creation strategist I had to exude wealth. I didn't want to go out and buy an expensive house with a large monthly mortgage payment, so I spend the extra money and rent nice hotel meeting rooms, and I still feed the guests. That way they can listen to what I am saying and see wealth around them at the hotel.

It's unfortunate that societal mindsets have been programmed to think that people have to show off wealth to prove that they know about wealth or are actually wealthy. In addition, being a black woman in a society where many have a negative overtone about black people (even other black people don't trust black people) I have to really work hard to make them see beyond color and the vehicle that I'm driving. My knowledge and strategies have to stand out.

The bottom line is this; In order to increase wealth in the church the mindsets of the congregation must be changed. The people must learn and understand that wealth is not in the homes, cars and clothes they buy. To a truly wealthy person most middle-class parishioners look foolish. We must take action and concentrate on true wealth and not showing off our hard work for some company somewhere.

WAYS TO INCREASE YOUR INCOME

When it comes down to increasing our income, we have to think about several factors. Some of these factors are:

How much extra time do I have to dedicate to increasing my income?

If you are already working 60 hours a week, you don't have a lot of time to add additional responsibilities. Some people work jobs that require more than the typical 9 to 5 schedule; for them to increase their income they can either:

- Ask the boss for a raise, which I don't recommend.
- Find other avenues of income while they are still on the job.
- Find another job with higher pay, while they are still working.
- Quit the current job and find another job, which I don't recommend.
- Quit the job to start a business, which I don't recommend.
- Start a business on the side and build it until the income from the business replaces the income from the job.

Asking for a raise or quitting one job and going to another with higher pay are only temporary fixes and may backfire on you due to layoffs and other factors beyond your control. Quitting a job before you find another job or quitting a job to start a brand-new business can get you into financial trouble because your bills are still due on a monthly basis.

What skills do I currently possess, or can I easily obtain, to help me increase my income?

If you have or can obtain skills that will get you a better job, a second job, or help you start a home-based business, you may want to consider these options. A computer operator with a demanding job and no time for family can start a computer service business on the weekends and grow the business to the point where he can fire his boss.

I have a friend who started and built his home-based business to the point where right before Christmas he went to work wearing a Santa Claus suit and told his boss, "I'm sorry but I'm going to have to fire you." He took down the large bag he had on his back and proceeded to give the boss and his co-workers gifts. Next, he walked out and never returned, because he almost tripled his annual income with his new home-based business.

Another example is someone who has a talent that they love. If you have a job that is totally different from the hobby that you love, you may be able to make a business out of that hobby and cash in on it. You may grow to the point that you don't have to work overtime, or you can quit your job altogether. We will talk about the potential for hobbies as businesses later.

What are the best ways for me to increase my income in the shortest amount of time?

If you are in debt, selecting a solution that will make your income increase as soon as possible will motivate you and boost your confidence. There are avenues out there that will have money in your pocket in days after getting started.

For couples; what can we do together to improve the household income?

A good way to increase income is for a couple to work together as a team and share in responsibilities in this quest. There are many couples that desire to find something to do together; it may be good for one of them to start off with a business that they both love, then quit the job and do the business full time. Later, the second spouse, who has been helping out during weekends and evenings, can quit their job after the business is consistently earning more than both of their salaries combined. This may sound far-fetched, but couples determined to grab hold of their financial futures are doing it all over the world.

Do I have any assets that I can put to work to help increase my income?

Some people have assets they can put to work or even sell to increase income. Have you taken the time to look through your house to find items that may increase your income? Do you have any old coins that may be of value? Do you have an old car that someone would be willing to buy and refurbish? What about old jewelry you no longer wear?

It may be to your benefit to search your house or your parents' house for things that may bring a little extra money to jump-start your finances.

I heard of a man who went to clean up the attic and found a box of old coins, which he took to a dealer and found out that he was sitting on over $20,000 in rare coins. I don't know what he did with the money, but that surely would have been enough to start a new business or an investment portfolio. There is a television show that values antiques that you may want to watch for great ideas about valuables around the house.

It should now be obvious that you need to get creative to find ways to increase your income if you are serious about fleeing the rat race!

DOES A FOR-PROFIT BUSINESS MAKE SENSE FOR ME?

I love non-profit organizations. They do a lot of good for the community. However, when it comes down to really achieving wealth, the for-profit business is the way to go. Pastors and congregants that start businesses have so much more potential to be debt free and financially free than the average worker will ever have. We don't have time to waste, we must be about Kingdom Advancement and that takes money, so the best thing for the church to do is build wealth. Proverbs 13:22 says that the wealth of the sinner is stored up for the righteous, so let's go get it and use it to make disciples in all nations!

Using a Job to Acquire Wealth

First off, you need to know something. Working a 9 to 5 job is not enough to build wealth. When I say 9 to 5, I mean any version of an 8 to 12-hour job at which you are working for someone else. Jobs are very necessary to make sure we don't shame the Lord by being debtors, but they usually only bring in enough to sustain the family. Church folks usually have jobs. Some make six-figures, and some make less than the U. S. poverty level of around $30,000 for a family of four.

I was recently asked by a young adult, "What does it really take to build wealth?" The conversation was centered around having a "good job" and I had to be the one to break the bad news to this kid, a job is not a path to wealth. It takes a lot more than that. I'm not knocking jobs, but I am saying that you need to be doing more than "working for the man" if you truly want to be wealthy.

When you have a job you're usually making someone else rich. Have you noticed that by the time you get paid; after taxes and other deductions and after your monthly bills you don't have much left, if anything? Do you realize that this is a plan that was hatched in the pit of hell?

I know people that make over $300,000 a year and some that make under $30,000 a year and both sets of people are constantly broke. It's not just about what you earn it's about what you keep, and what you do with what you keep. You have to become your own boss and buy back your time from the grind. Even if you keep the job you must use all of your earnings wisely.

Start from Where You are with What You Have

Some people have asked me how I went from rock bottom to climbing my way out and pressing through.

When I came home from the prison camp I had a minimum wage job and almost immediately I was in the process of getting a divorce. But I also had determination to rise above my circumstances.

I had always heard from the elders to do the best you can with what you have, so I assessed what I had physically, mentally, spiritually, and socially, and I took what I had, the money from that minimum wage job, and started to build a business.

People always look around at other people and at the television and think they have nothing to offer. But when they really think about it, God gave them gifts and these gifts can be used to gain wealth and grow the Kingdom.

For example, there was a Christian woman who took the money from her job and bought stainless steel pots and pans because she is a great cook. She found a commercial kitchen that she could rent (it's illegal in most places to sell food made from your home) and she started cooking great healthy meals while at the same time having a family member video record her doing the preparation. She talked to people about her healthy meals and started to acquire high-end clients who had money but didn't want to cook.

Instead of spending the money on clothes and shoes, she invested the funds in professional video recording equipment, and used the videos shot by a family member to perfect her on-camera style. Soon she was a hit in the local high-end community. She increased her prices for meals based on the high demand and started selling meal preparation videos. She was eventually able to pay off her home, at which time she quit her low paying job and became a full-time business owner. This woman is now a six-figure business owner who makes money in her sleep because people are buying her videos online around the clock from around the world. She also has a few high-end clients for which she prepares meals and caters events. She is no longer trading hours for dollars. This can be you or any of the people in your church if they really want it.

Here are your first three questions to write down and answer IN WRITING if you want to start where you are with what you have:

- WHAT DO I WANT?
- WHY DO I WANT IT? (Why is it important to me?)
- WHAT AM I WILLING TO GIVE UP TO GET IT?

Stop Falling for Distractions

Now, let's talk about distractions. So many people don't understand that most of the media out there these days is created to distract you from being who you are supposed to be. All the major television stations, cable stations, sports and non-reality shows, and social media eat up thousands of hours of your time. Statistics say that the average teen spends nine hours a day on social media and the average adult spends five hours a day watching TV. Television makes you stupid—really! Even the "best" TV shows are only at middle school levels. Mark Twain got it right when he observed that, "If you don't read the newspapers you are uninformed . . . but if you do read the newspapers you are misinformed!" Unfortunately, those that call themselves Christians fall right into this trap and are part of these statistics.

I was actually astounded when I read these facts and it made me understand, all the more, why people are stuck in the earn-spend cycle. You know what that is don't you? It's when people get paid on Friday, go straight to the Mall and buy the brand-named clothes and shoes, go partying Friday and Saturday night, come to church all sleepy Sunday morning and drop $5 in the bucket, and after paying rent, car note, and insurance they are BROKE until the next paycheck when they do it all over again. You know exactly what I'm talking about!

We need to get church folks to stop falling for the master plan to keep us in the earn/spend slave mode and commit to turning off the TV and social media for a while. When we do that, we don't just lie down, we need to study and meditate on God's word so that we will always be in line with His plan for our lives. We also need to study wealthy people so that we will know how to gain, manage, and keep wealth.

Starting a Home-Based Business

My biggest investment is in myself, not the stock market, bonds, mutual funds, IRAs, or 401Ks. I don't trust other people to take care of my money and I don't put money into anything that can disappear in the blink of an eye! Truth be told all that stuff is rigged anyway. If you do a little research you'll find that I'm not kidding. You saw what happened in September 2008! Think it won't happen again?

What DO I have confidence in? The Word of God and his gift to us in being able to create. One of those creations is the financial wonder called the Home-Based Business!

I believe that having a home-based business is key to the success of the church in growing and maturing disciples.

Many churches that are financially stable have entrepreneurial programs that:

- Teach members business principals
- Bring in successful business people (saved and unsaved) to teach the members how to operate businesses
- Teach the ethics of being a Christian in business.

Pastors and church members can start with a minimum investment and operate from a spare bedroom or a garage. If they don't like the business they started, they haven't sold the family farm. They can quit and start over.

Also, the Internet and computer and communication technologies now offer home-based entrepreneurs the same tools to operate as those used by multi-national corporations, so saints can make money from all over the world in their sleep.

But the best thing about having a home-based business is the tax reduction. Someone that has a home-based business can deduct part of their cell phone bill, Internet, mileage, and other expenses. Someone that doesn't have a business is still paying for the same expenses, but they don't get a dime in deductions for them.

The Trump tax law even gives small business owners additional deductions that weren't available before. I just pray that they keep these tax advantages in place for decades to come.

I recommend that everyone start a home-based business instead of starting a brick and mortar business because you don't want to start off in the hole, renting a separate space for a business. You will have more money and flexibility when you start from home.

I know lots of people making six and even seven figures from home. Some are part-time business owners, and some are full time. The common denominator is that they all work hard and invest in themselves instead of a failed system. Think about starting an entrepreneurial program at your church if you don't have one already. If you have a program in place enhancing it may increase attendance, business knowledge and giving.

A Typical Tax Strategy of the Wealthy

Now I'm going to reward the business owners with a great tax tip. It won't apply to everyone, but it will apply to some of you.

If you have employees in your home-based business, you'll have to pay them wages and withhold federal, state, social security tax and Medicare tax on the employees.

However, you can employ your children that are between the ages of 6 and 18, pay them wages of up to the standard deduction ($12,000 is the standard deduction for single people for the 2018 tax return) and pay no tax at all!

This means that if you have two children between 6 and 18 you can pay them $12,000 each in 2018 and have a $24,000 deduction for your business on your Schedule C business Profit and Loss Statement.

For example, if you have a 13-year-old and a 16-year-old, you may have them sweep the office, take out the garbage, shred papers, answer the phone, greet your clients at the door and a host of other tasks. You were already buying them designer clothes, video games and expensive gym shoes. Now, they can pay for these items with their own wages while you get a nice tax deduction.

You may even pay your children, let them gift the payments back to you and you use the funds for a down payment on a home or investment property, for college tuition or for advertising to grow your business even more!

Another strategy that wealthy people use is to pay the children, have the children go out and buy equipment for the business then lease the equipment to your company, so that they can have perpetual rental income even beyond their 18th birthday while you get to deduct their salary and the rental expense for renting the equipment from them. In this instance either you or the children WILL have to pay tax, but it will be worth it to utilize these strategies that wealthy people use regularly!

Of course, I'm simplifying this for time sake, and there are strict rules to this great benefit. First, you must actually pay the children and keep timesheets; and they must actually work. This can't be just a paper transaction. You need to pay them by check and they need to deposit these checks into their own personal savings or checking accounts. Next, you must fill out the proper payroll tax returns each quarter. Instead of paying payroll tax, however, you write in "exempt student" and put zero for the tax.

Do more research on this deduction if you qualify and I pray that you are able to use it to keep more of what you earn in the family.

SAVING AND INVESTING FOR THE CHURCH

So, what is the best way for the church to save and invest? I'll share some ideas and strategies that I have seen and/or used. But first we need to get some definitions clear.

Saving

Once you have started to reduce your expenses and increase your income it's time to start saving. Saving is defined as putting money away in, for example, a deposit account, a pension account, an investment account, or in cash. Saving also involves reducing expenses, such as credit card debt.

Why Should I Save?

Believe it or not some people don't understand the necessity of saving and others don't believe that they need to save. No wonder so many people are constantly living on the poverty line and so many churches are struggling. When my children wanted to spend all of their allowance I wouldn't let them. I bought both of them three-drawer boxes and made them give 15%, save 35% and then they could spend 50%. They didn't like that rule and asked me why they had to save. I let them know that there would be times that some special event was presented to them, or an opportunity to take a trip, and if they didn't have any money they would miss out.

I turned into my father and told them that luck is when preparation and opportunity meet, and being prepared often involves having the money to take advantage of a given opportunity.

It is my understanding that Conrad Hilton purchased many of his starter hotels during the depression at fire sale rates because he had the cash. From there everything is history. During the depression of 2008 and for a few years following, there were thousands of people that were able to purchase real estate for pennies on the dollar because they had savings. Not all of these were rich people. I know of a couple that had been saving for a modest home and making sure that they were working towards being debt free. They planned to purchase a three-bedroom home in a decent middle-class neighborhood. However, right after the crash when the housing market tanked, they were able to purchase a five-bedroom home in an upscale neighborhood for the same down payment and monthly payments they would have paid for the smaller home a few years earlier. Someone that had not saved and was living from hand to mouth in a large home had to sell it and lose all of their equity in the house in order to avoid foreclosure and bankruptcy.

Savings are also essential because they help you avoid using credit for purchases. People that spend all that they earn end up using credit cards and loans for so-called emergencies—like new tires, replacement appliances, repairs, and funeral expenses. This is the money you put aside for future expenditures that may occur in the next three to fifteen years. For example, I have an associate that decided to go to graduate school. Because she saved lots of money she was able to be a full-time student and live off of her savings for the entire degree program instead of taking out student loans. You also want to save for vacations. I know so many people that take vacations using credit cards and loans. They may have had a nice time for a week or even two, however, when they return home the bills start arriving in the mail, causing stress and diminishing the value and memory of their vacation. One other very important reason to save is in case of financial disaster. We never want financial calamity to strike our families, and we pray that it doesn't. However, sometimes bad things happen. If you have saved money for "a rainy day" then your family stability can be kept intact. For example, I have a relative that lost his job during the depression of 2008. Because he had diligently saved his money he was able to live for two years until a new job came along. He didn't have to borrow or use credit cards during that time. If you've saved money for things that don't occur often and for financial tragedy, your diligence will save you from paying interest on loans and credit cards, keep your credit score high and give you peace of mind.

How Should I Save?

I believe that you need at least three "savings pots." I like having a short-term savings pot, a mid-term savings pot, and a long-term savings pot. At this time, I think it's prudent to explain the difference between saving and investing. When I mention the long-term savings pot people often mistake this pot for investing but this is not the case.

The purpose of saving is to safeguard that set-aside money—the money for emergencies and planned short-term expenses like vacations or college. The purpose of investing is to grow the money that you have put away. Invested funds are above and beyond the amount you need for future expenditures and possible financial disaster. In essence, the savings pots will be used at some point in the near future or up to 15 years out, but it will be used for planned expenses. The investments are put aside to constantly and consistently grow so that you can live off of those funds and their earnings even when you are no longer physically working.

Now that we have discussed the difference between saving and investing let's discuss the different savings pots.

Short-Term Savings Pot

I believe that the short-term savings pot is something that you can save in a hidden place in your home. The short-term pot may be up to around $6,000 and will cover some of the following items:

- Tire replacement
- Major auto repairs (timing belt)
- Vacations
- Emergency travel (funerals)
- Appliance repairs and replacement (air conditioners, water heaters)

Mid-Term Savings Pot

These funds should be absolutely safe but not kept in your home because of the amount of funds. A bank CD is an option but understand that you will not be earning any significant amounts of interest on the funds. These funds should be used to accelerate debt payoff and to keep handy in case you need to buy large items like used cars. The mid-term savings pot may be up to around $12,000 and will cover some of the following items:

- Paying off a small credit card
- Buying a good used car

- Large home repair (roof repair)
- Long-term or international vacations (Mediterranean cruise)
- Six months of living expenses in case of a medical or other calamity

Long-Term Savings Pot

The long-term savings should also be absolutely safe. These funds may be placed in a Money Market Account or some other account/instrument that is (1) liquid and you have the ability to access it within 72 hours or less and (2) earning some type of interest above what a regular bank savings account pays, (note that "regular bank savings accounts" used to pay substantial dividends, however due to massive government/banker fraud against the saving public, these accounts now pay essentially ZERO interest to citizen savers). These funds should cover very large future expected or unexpected expenditures. The long-term savings pot will be more than $15,000 and will cover some of the following items:

- A new car (good used car or truck)
- College tuition
- Retirement home
- Medical bills not covered by insurance
- Living expenses in case of a job loss
- Other family adversity

Where Should I Save?

This money should <u>not</u> be put in stocks, bonds, or mutual funds because they are dangerous—this is because their values can change drastically without notice due to events of which the ordinary investor will have no warning . . . until it is too late. If you don't believe that go back and look at news stories from September 2008. The value of stocks slipped back into pre-1930 values after the depression of 2008 and even though the financial gurus are telling you that the market has recovered it's only pumping up for another crash in the future. Your savings and investments should be kept far from the digital forms of investing and put into hard assets. Why?

Here's why. Today's trading markets are Not your grandfather's markets when personal contacts and inside information (legal and illegal) were the keys to fortunes. Today you will be competing against (very) sophisticated computers running (very) sophisticated software with reams of up to the second legal and illegal inside information. If you are in doubt, do yourself a favor. Pick up a commercially available checkers and/or chess program and play against the computer. If the program is any good at all you will NEVER win, so how could you expect to prevail against systems with hundreds of times better computers, software, and information than you will have.

For the savings pots you may want to keep some in a money market account, or a special college fund that lets you take the money out tax-free for tuition, but that's as far as I would personally go. I have some of my savings in gold and silver, some in cash and some in negotiable instruments (A negotiable instrument is a document guaranteeing the payment of a specific amount of money, either on demand, or at a set time, with the payer named on the document). Investments will be discussed in the next section.

Note that when these funds are diminishing in any category you must immediately begin to replenish them before they are depleted. Also, savings pots should never be invested in stocks, bonds, or retirement funds because you can't take the chance of seeing your funds disappear like they did in 2008; you won't have time to recover!

INVESTING

Where Is the Road to Wealth? Here Is the Road to Wealth.

High Risk/Speculative Investments (Last)
Capital/Guaranteed—Low-Risk Investments
Emergency Funds—Three Months of Household Expenses
Insurance (Health & Life)/Assurance—Six Months of Expenses

Your stair step to financial freedom can be found above. If you follow this model and the other rules in this book, before you know it you will be stress-free and on your way to the winner's circle. If congregations are taught these principles the church will be debt free and would be able to open their own banks!

Let's start out on the bottom with Insurance and Assurance.

Insurance is self-explanatory. It is good to have life and health insurance as well as home, auto, and any other insurance that will help you in times of need. Make sure that you shop around for the best prices as you have learned to do in this book. There are many Internet sites that will give you quotes on all types of insurance coverages. Take time to research so that your expenses will be low, and your coverage will be good.

It's essential that the church have the necessary insurance to ensure that it doesn't have to close its doors due to some unforeseen circumstances. It's very dangerous to think that nothing will ever happen and not have the proper insurance policies in place. Here are some types of insurances churches need:

- General Liability
- Key Man—life insurance on the pastor and maybe associate pastors
- Automobile
- Property Damage and Fire
- Counseling
- Sexual Abuse & Molestation
- Missions Trip

Assurance means that you have saved six months of living expenses in case of some disaster. If you can't work for six months but all the bills are still due, how much would you need to make sure that you won't fall into financial ruin? If your household income and expenses are $3,000 per month, you can see that you would need to save $18,000 in Assurance. You need to keep this money very liquid. One clever strategy is to purchase three bank CDs for $6,000 each as you accumulate the $6,000 increments. Purchase three-month CDs three months in a row, so that one will mature every three months and you will have your expenses taken care of in case of emergency. Keep the funds in any liquid means that you want, although I don't recommend keeping that kind of cash under your bed.

As far as assurance funds for the church are concerned, saving at least six months of operating capital is a good start to making sure the church doesn't meet with sudden disaster. I know that many churches don't collect enough in tithes and offerings to make that happen, but I would recommend saving at least six months of mortgage payments in a safe vehicle or even the church's secure safe, just in case it's needed.

Emergency Funds. This is an unreal term, because we really don't have that many emergencies. You know that those tires will be bald soon, and you know that elderly relatives will pass away; these are not unexpected occurrences or emergencies.

Many people tell me that the reason they are in debt is because they had several emergencies and that they had to charge their credit card to the max. When I asked what the emergencies were, they told me things like:

- "My transmission blew," but you knew you had 315,000 miles on that truck and that it was time for some maintenance.
- "Aunt Lula Mae passed away and I had to get a flight to the funeral and because it was last minute, the flight was $1,000 and I had to charge it on my Visa," but you knew Aunt Lula Mae and all of her sisters are elderly and you should have put travel money aside for the funerals.
- "I needed a vacation because I was under a lot of stress, so I charged a 7-day Caribbean cruise on my card," and you came back more in debt and under more stress!

We can't keep using excuses to hide our lack of planning. Put three to six months of living expenses away for irregular occurrences to keep from racking up credit card debt and interest.

Estimate a monthly amount in all of your expense categories based on what you spent last year, then add additional categories for your family, and multiply by 12 for the annual estimates. Take that annual total to see how much per month you will need to put aside for emergencies. If three months of living expenses is not enough, add additional months as needed.

For example, the Duncan family likes to take vacations. They have totaled up their so-called emergency expenses and determined that they need $14,373 per year to take care of things other than household expenses. Their lifestyle requires that they either set aside $1,197 per month for this fund or cut down on their vacations and other noted expenses. If they continue to fund these irregular expenses without planning for them, they will fall deep into debt.

Credit card debt is the most popular way to get deep in debt. Churches can easily get into credit card debt also.

So, stop using them for things you can't afford to pay for in cash! The church needs to very carefully use any credit that it has been granted because, as Scripture says in Proverbs 22:7, "The rich rules over the poor, and the borrower is servant to the lender."

Capital Guaranteed Investments

Capital guaranteed investments simply mean that if you put a certain amount into the investment; you will at least get that amount back. These investments are available in the states and offshore, but they are rare. We will talk a little more about offshore investing in our section about what the wealthy do. However, some of us have noticed that the "powers that be" and the news media try to scare the middle-class away from even thinking about investing internationally by associating everything offshore with something illegal. If you put on your thinking caps, you will see that all of the wealthy families, including high level politicians; the Rockefellers, Carnegies, Fords, and Kennedys have millions of dollars invested offshore directly and indirectly. If you look at what they are doing, how can you be scared into keeping your funds in losing instruments here in the States?

Investments that are capital guaranteed are better for the beginner investor who can't afford to lose what has been invested. A good investment coach will tell you, "Never invest what you can't afford to lose." Many of us have been shell-shocked by smooth-talking investment gurus in Italian suits, telling us that their investment will gain us 5% per month. There are investments in the marketplace that will bring those kinds of returns; however, your job is to investigate and research these investments instead of just throwing your wallet at the person with the smooth presentation.

Doing your research and finding capital guaranteed investments at the start of your investment experience will keep you on the road to wealth without any sidetracks, such as those with pie in the sky numbers that make you lose your investment funds.

One capital guaranteed/low risk (usually) investment is real estate. Real estate has recently come out of a free fall in the States, and it's no longer easy to get bottom basement prices on decent houses for rental property. But I'm sure that with research you can find a deal.

As far as real estate in the United States, there are only a few types of rental property that I would purchase. One is a small two-bedroom home near a college campus. I feel that I would have near 100% occupancy, even during the summer, if I had such a property. Another real estate investment that I would make is in a daycare center/building in or very close to an upper-middle-class neighborhood. I feel that the daycare center would have near capacity year-round and I would have no problem collecting rent from the center directors.

When I mentioned this scenario in a workshop once, a participant asked me if I would consider owning the daycare center itself. I had to think about it but eventually I answered that I would own a daycare center in that environment only under a few choice scenarios. The daycare center would have to be unique in more than one way; for example, it would have to offer multiple languages to the older children, it would have to have medical staff and it would have to be a 24-hour center. Those qualities would make it unique enough that there would be a waiting list for enrollment. I went on to state that I would eventually grow it into a dynamic private school. I believe that is a great idea for a church school and would bring more people into the church and thus bring more people to Christ.

Real estate in other countries is another option that many in the United States, even real estate agents and brokers, have not looked into. Countries like Costa Rica, Panama, Ecuador, and Chile are booming, and because of their low cost of living and the warm weather, many retirees from all over the world rush in to buy land in these places.

Look into real estate deals in areas in the United States in areas that are not on the decline, but also look closely at international real estate.

When purchasing abroad you must learn the rules because they operate very differently in many countries. In some countries, a realtor can sell the seller's house for a higher list price, give the seller what he asked for, and keep the rest!

I have friends who purchased a home in Panama, only to have the agent tell them, one day before they left St. Louis to move down there, that their home was sold to someone else for $95,000 more than they contracted for, even though they put a down payment on the home and signed a contract! They received their down payment back, but they had to find another home, which took them two additional months!

As I write this book I am purchasing property on the Caribbean coast of Costa Rica. The area had not been developed like the west coast, and it is ripe for a myriad of investment opportunities including rental real estate, restaurants, medical practices, and other businesses. I feel like I am reaping an opportunity similar to what it was like to have invested in Hawaii in the 1960s!

Speculative Investments

Speculative (high risk) investments are just that. These are the high yield; high-risk investments that are offered mostly by companies that only deal with accredited investors.

Accredited Investors are people who have a million dollars net worth (excluding the value of a primary residence), or who earn $200,000 per year as a single person or $300,000 as a married couple. This designation, developed by the Securities and Exchange Commission (SEC), keeps the middle-class from excelling in income investments. By deciding that middle-class people are not smart enough to research and invest with wisdom, the SEC forbids investment brokers and investment advisors from showing high yield investments to people who don't meet the criteria. Even if you have great investment knowledge, you can't invest in certain investments if you don't earn $200,000 a year and you don't have one million dollars net worth. This is wrong on so many different levels that I just have to stop right here before I get angry all over again. Stock and investment brokers, who are licensed and regulated by the SEC and the National Association of Securities Dealers (NASD), can have you in their office selling you on IRAs and Mutual Funds, and the very next hour have another couple in their office selling them high-yield investments that you will never know about. Not all of these investments are high-risk, but you still can't know about them!

Another high yield investment strategy is to become a small venture capitalist who loans funds to small up and coming businesses that prove that they will make a profit. This method takes serious research. I know two men that make a living investing in companies that show great potential. They do the research and if they can make money investing in these small companies, they invest and reap large dividends, as opposed to throwing money into mutual funds that include failing companies that they know nothing about. The church is not allowed to participate in this type of investment, but individuals can take advantage of them.

There are many ways for you to take advantage of some of these higher yield investments even when you have the funds but are not an accredited investor, and I will discuss those options in the next section of the book when we talk about what the wealthy do to become and stay wealthy. Speculative investments should be your last step, though; like it does for the wealthy, this is where your money makes money.

QUESTIONS YOU NEED TO ASK BEFORE INVESTING

I talked earlier about how people go to investment seminars, get caught up in the hype of the smooth-talking presenter and throw their wallets open, often without asking any questions about the investment being offered. Before you invest anything, you need to ask these questions:

What is being offered/what is the product? If the presenter can't explain this clearly and in detail, you may want to turn away. I attended an investment conference in Cancun and another attendee had done his homework to the point that he ran circles around the presenter with his questions. I was embarrassed for the presenter, and she was as red as an apple by the end of her presentation. Needless to say, none of the attendees invested in the product that she was offering.

Why do they need my money? Often, they really don't! Others could fund the opportunity they present, or they may have squandered money previously invested. In either case, you want to find out how much money the company has spent, and how the company spent it.

Who is in charge? You always want to know who is at the helm of the product or service being presented. The presenter at an investment conference in Greece was the actual product inventor and developer; he had put his life into the product, and I could feel his passion. He was an engineer and he did a great job developing and presenting the product, and I felt very comfortable with that investment opportunity.

Do they make money even if I don't? I don't invest in the stock market or use stockbrokers, because they make me broker and broker. Whenever others make money whether you make any or not, you are going down a dangerous road. Often when you trade stock, the broker earns money on every trade. Also, stock and insurance brokers earn differing commissions on different products, so they may offer you an inferior product just to receive a higher commission.

How much money does the presenter personally have invested? Presentations made by salespeople are turnoffs to me; I want to hear from the owner, founder, or an officer who has a personal stake in the product or service. These are the people who have the real knowledge necessary to make prudent investment decisions. In my previous example, the presenter was a saleswoman who knew less than the attendee, and it showed when she couldn't answer questions that someone more intimately involved with the company would have been able to answer.

What market factors drive the amount of projected return? Market factors such as interest rates, economic growth, trade and capital flows, and merger and acquisition activity affect the amount of return you may receive on an investment. In addition, some products are manufactured in different places of the world. You need to know where the products are made and the political climate in that area. I lost thousands in an investment based in a South American country when corporate greed and government corruption tied the company's hands and stopped production. Who knows whether I will ever regain my principal investment? As of this writing there may be chance. Because the presenter of that investment opportunity has her life tied up in the investment she is still fighting in court and it has been over 18 years!

What is the company's background? How long has it been in business? The shorter the amount of time a company has been in business, the riskier the investment.

New companies need to work out their glitches before you invest substantial amounts of money; they need to earn your trust by showing growth and profits. Make sure that when you ask this question the answer includes only the amount of time the company has existed in its current state. I have heard presenters give longer existence dates for companies that started out with other names, but failed and re-opened with a new name. Many companies don't want you to know that they have a checkered past.

Will all or part of my invested principal be at risk? Earlier, we discussed capital guaranteed investments, in which you are guaranteed to get back at least what you invested. Some guarantee only to return part of your investment should there be problems or loss involved. Make sure you know the entire story and exactly how much is guaranteed and get it in writing!

Can I or any other investors visit the company's facility? This is an important question, as some "fake" companies operate out of a private mailbox address, or even from someone's home. People tend not to invest in companies that don't have a brick-and-mortar presence, and some organizations try to hide the fact that they are small by renting a private mailbox on a busy street. I have seen some of them bring pictures of their supposed facility, which turned out to be pictures of someone else's business. Before many of my friends invest, they pay a visit to the company and have a talk with the partners and officers. Even if a partner or officer presented the investment, the investor validates concerns by visiting the actual facility and seeing the work in progress.

How often do investors receive updates and payments? When you are considering an investment, you need to know the company's policies and procedures. You want to know how often you will receive updates about your investment; some companies send out monthly or quarterly newsletters, while others only contact investors once a year. You also want to know when you will be paid; some investments pay out monthly or quarterly. I have heard about investments that paid out after five years and usually offer a higher rate of return because they have your money so long. If you want a long-term investment to generate college tuition for your teenager, this may be the way to go.

What is the exit strategy to recoup all of my funds? You should always know where the exits are when you are in a building and when you invest. If you don't ask, you may find out the hard way that you can't get your money back or at least not before a certain date. If you invest in a product that has a high rate of return and claims that you will receive full principal and interest in five years, will you be able to get the principal back after two years if you fall on hard times, or will you forfeit part of the principal and interest earned by taking the money out early? You need to ask the hard questions, or you might end up in a bad predicament. If someone asked these questions during "slick" presentations, most people in the audience would never invest unless the answers were true and acceptable.

I said all that about high-risk investments, but wealthy people put little into them. Wealthy people invest in "high-yield low-risk" investments. While hanging around wealthy people I've learned some once classified information concerning wealth. This information permits wealthy people to stay that way. What I learned is that wealthy people only use a small percentage of their money on speculative investments. They first create and grow a strong financial foundation that's secure and virtually totally protected against losses. Then they do research and find companies and opportunities in which to invest. Sometimes these investments are "long shots" and if they fail all of the invested funds are lost. However, if the investments pay off they bring high returns and the wealthy use part of these high returns to invest in other opportunities that are considered speculative. Wealthy people invest most of their money in companies and opportunities that they are familiar with, as opposed to throwing money into the stock market. They start businesses, take over good businesses with bad management and replace the management, and they constantly research to find solid opportunities. These investments bring them consistent cash flow, and if they decide to sell a company that they have started they usually earn millions of dollars.

From now on we as the Body of Christ must make sure that we carefully research before we invest, or we will not be able to climb the stairs to wealth without falling backward.

How Do the Wealthy Stay Wealthy?

First, we need to define wealth so that we are all on the same page. The best definition that I have heard for financial wealth is this: Wealth is determined by the number of days you can survive without working, or anyone else in your household physically working and still maintain (or increase) your standard of living.

That definition kicks out people who have a lot of stuff but would lose it all in a month or two if they could not work to keep that stuff.

There are literally millions of people in the US with luxury cars, homes, vacation homes, and all of the latest gadgets who would lose it all in a matter of months if there were a job loss, divorce, medical catastrophe, or something of that nature. These people are not wealthy, and they never were. Wealthy people make money on their money and have multiple streams of income so that they can go on for years or for the rest of their lives without physically having to work. This is your achievable goal if you follow the principles and the rules you have learned.

We all want financial freedom. My favorite definition of financial freedom is: **The ability to do what you love, when you want, with whomever you want, with no concern about money.** In order for you to have the time to do what you want and have no concern about money, you have to get to work on your strategy right away. Christians need to learn how to buy back their time from jobs and other activities that they have no control over.

Let me tell you the secrets of the wealthy. They have been teaching me for many years now because they found that I was not only willing to learn, but willing to listen and implement the strategies they shared. They realized that they were not throwing their pearls before swine, and

I gleaned an abundance of knowledge from them, for which I'm truly grateful.

Wealthy people buy assets, not liabilities. They don't just rent a building for an office; they buy a building, put their office in it, and rent out the other suites so that their tenants pay the mortgage for the entire building, usually without knowing that one of them owns the building! Wealthy people buy or form profitable businesses. Instead of buying big cars and homes they can't afford to pay cash for, they wait until the business income is enough to pay for the cars and homes, or they get loans at low interest rates and pay the loans off with funds that are earning a higher interest rate. They let the company buy the cars they drive and the homes in which they live. I have learned that wealthy people endeavor to own nothing, but control everything through corporations, trusts, foundations, and international businesses.

Wealthy people's assets grow based on the formula for compound interest and they become wealthier. They use money that has been passively earned through investments, and their assets pay for their liabilities. If they want a new house, they use the earnings from an investment to get that property. They will purchase rental property, and when it is fully paid for (via the rental income), they will use that rental income to pay for their new home or additional rental property. When they utilize these strategies, their time is their own to use as they see fit; they find more ways for their money to make money, instead of working ten hours a day only to come home to watch the ballgame. They become powerful and influential; people with money-making opportunities introduce them to more opportunities because they are able to fund their deals. As these opportunities roll in and, after research, they take advantage of them; they build wealth and multiple income streams very quickly.

One of the most important things about wealthy people is that they teach their children HOW TO HAVE MONEY WORK FOR THEM, not how to work for money. They start their children off young, teaching them that they can make money without working for other people.

Many wealthy people have their very young children involved in the family business, and even Internet businesses. So, while the children are asleep on a Tuesday night, they are making money because someone on the other side of the country or the other side of the world is buying that product. That child will learn the definition of "mailbox/inbox money" when they receive checks in the mail or have funds earned in their business downloaded to a prepaid debit card or to their bank account. These children can earn thousands of dollars before even reaching high school; and be determined to always make "mailbox/inbox money" instead of working for a paycheck. Our children can learn these same principles and use these same tactics if we just teach them.

Don't get me wrong—cutting grass and babysitting are fine, but wealthy people teach their children how to operate on a global level, and you need to start learning how and teaching your children the same thing! These are the future leaders of the church and they will know how to efficiently operate as a Christian business if taught early.

Wealthy people also make sure their children receive a good practical, hands-on education and work in their business, instead of watching TV or playing too many sports and video games. They tell the children that they will have to work now in order to receive a share of the family business later, which gives them incentive to work hard and learn the business, like Donald Trump learned from his father, and the Rockefellers and many other wealthy children learned from their families.

Wealthy people create their own reality, and if something in their environment is not to their liking, they have the money and power to change it. They find and utilize the resources they need to accomplish their goals and dreams. The wealthy are not limited by conventional thinking or the perceived limitations of the masses. Many people limit themselves with excuses and things that happened to them in the past. Wealthy people do not let obstacles stop them; they move the obstacle, destroy it, or buy it!

The bottom line is that whatever wealthy people can conceive, they can achieve, and this is the mindset that we all need to develop in order to become wealthy. The wealth that we create should be used as a means to fund Christianity worldwide.

Some of the things we are not taught in the public school system but that wealthy people know and teach their children are listed below.

How to Keep the Money We Earn

Control spending. As discussed earlier, middle-class people are in an earn/spend cycle and as long as that is the case, they will never become wealthy. Wealthy people control their spending and utilize the age-old principle of delayed gratification. My father taught me about delayed gratification when I was eight years old, when he told me that if I saved my little allowance instead of buying candy or toys, I would later be able to get nicer things, like a bike or the archery set that I wanted.

Wealthy children learn about delayed gratification, unlike many children not born wealthy. We need to get back to showing our children the value of saving for things instead of always having their hands out. We ourselves need to learn that the mall isn't the place to be when we are in debt! Also, we as adults need to practice delayed gratification daily.

HOW TO RESEARCH WHERE TO INVEST OUR EARNINGS

Stop taking financial advice from financially illiterate people. People will listen to—and throw money at—someone with the hottest stock tip, who may be broker than a panhandler.

You need to pay attention to who advises you. If the people you learn about wealth from aren't wealthy or rapidly heading toward wealth, then you need to start listening to those who are wealthy and those who are on the path to wealth.

HOW TO KEEP OTHER PEOPLE AWAY FROM THE MONEY THAT WE EARN

Avoid contingency litigation and frivolous lawsuits. Our country is one of the few that will let one person sue another without paying a bond up front.

A lawyer can take a case on contingency, which means that they get paid ***after*** they get a judgment, which many so-called third-world countries don't even allow.

In some countries you have to put up a $25,000 bond in order to sue someone, and if you lose, the $25,000 goes toward the defendant's attorney fees and/or loss of work dealing with the case! Over half of the lawsuits would surely stop if that were the law in the U.S.; however, since most legislators are also lawyers, we have as much chance of getting rid of contingency litigation as I have of winning the lottery, which I have never played.

The Su-nited States has 5% of the world's population and:

- 70% of the world's attorneys
- 94% of world's lawsuits
- 80,000 law school graduates annually
- 100,000,000 cases per year
- A new lawsuit filed every 30 seconds
- Each American bears a 1 in 3 chance of being sued
- More law students than lawyers

With that in mind, it is suspect that asset protection is not a big part of the education of the middle-class, while the wealthy have been using asset protection strategies since the early 1900s and before. When someone dies and has a few assets that they thought were going to be given to their loved ones, the loved ones are in for a shock if the proper steps have not been taken to protect the assets. For instance, the average time to probate an estate is about fifteen months! Because lawyers or trustees often get involved and sometimes draw the process out, the average loss to an estate is 30%. is means that if someone left $100,000 to split between four people, and did not take proper asset protection steps, each heir will get only $17,500 instead of $25,000, which would make a difference for anyone in the middle-class! The probate business generates $25 billion annually, but as we educate ourselves on proper asset protection, that amount will shrink significantly.

Have you ever wondered why the Rockefeller and Carnegie families have had land and other wealth for hundreds of years, while your family members die and leave bills? Have you ever wondered why the Kennedys never lose a lawsuit? Wealthy people use business structures (trusts, limited liability companies, foundations, and international business corporations) to protect their assets from lawsuits, divorce, and other factors that may interfere with the perpetuity of their family legacies. Although that discussion is beyond the scope of this book, suffice it to say that when you get out of debt and start to invest, you will want to research these important ways to keep what you earn, protect it, and make it grow. Pastors and church administrators really need to learn these strategies because people at your church may want to leave a gift or endowment to the church and someone on staff will need to know how to record it and what to do when the time comes to collect it. Many wealthy people leave thousands of dollars to church through investment vehicles and trust accounts. Be knowledgeable in this arena so that you can be a worthy beneficiary of these funds. It may even be a good idea to have an expert on asset protection and life-long giving come to your church and present these concepts to the congregation. You never know, some of your members may have funds to give and may need to know how to leave funds to the church and receive the greatest benefit (tax wise) from the gift.

How to Have Your Money Work for You so that You Don't Have to Work for Money.

We are not taught to become **knowledgeable investors** because many of the wealthy want to keep these secrets for themselves. Consequently, these strategies are rarely taught, even at the university level.

We are not taught to create **passive income streams;** one of the main things we need to learn in order to have our money earn money. We can get involved in businesses that will generate passive income streams and invest in profitable ventures. We will discuss this area shortly. We are not taught to create profitable systems or follow **profitable systems** that are already in place. A profitable system is one which, once set up, requires little oversight and maintenance, so that you can go on vacation and the system will continue to work in your absence.

An excellent example of a profitable system is the restaurant franchise system. When you purchase a Chick-Fil-A franchise, you receive unchangeable rules and regulations. Their system has proven to be profitable; even if you take a month-long sabbatical, you will still expect to earn profits in your absence. This scenario is not so when you have a job, or when you are self-employed.

Let me quickly explain the difference between owning a business and being self-employed. When you are self-employed, you own a job, as opposed to having a job working for someone else. The key differentiator between being self-employed and owning a business is downtime. When someone is self-employed, and they get ill or go on vacation, there is no money coming in. When someone has a business and they get sick or go on a vacation, money is still flowing into their bank account. I explained this fact in all of my workshops because I need everyone to understand the difference. Once during a workshop an old friend stood up and said, "I need to tell my brother this. He always runs around telling everyone that he owns his own business. But when he gets sick he has no money coming in and he comes asking to borrow money from me until he gets up and running again!"

In contrast, the owner of a Chic-Fil-A franchise can take a month-long vacation and as long as she has left a good manager behind the store will continue to run smoothly and money will continue to flow into the bank account.

Once Christians study and find the profitable systems that suit our personalities, skills, time, and lifestyles we will be another step closer to escaping the rat race and being freed up enough to spend most of our time working in ministry instead of for "the man".

Proper Business Structuring

Managing a business and having a job are truly like night and day. When a person has a job or is self-employed (receiving the Form1099), he/she will be expected to pay lots of taxes. So, that cycle goes like this:

EARN—TAX—SPEND

However, when a small business or corporation makes money there is a different outcome. They earn money then they spend the money first, on ordinary and necessary business expenses, and anything left over is taxed. For example, a corporation will have expenses such as the company car, company travel, and paying the manager's mother to answer the phone for extra income. Businesses have been utilizing these strategies for decades, while the middle-class pays out everything and is broke, busted, and disgusted at the end of each month.

As you start your business, you may want to first structure it so that you own nothing and control everything as the Rockefellers do, and so that you know how to add other structures (Limited Liability Companies, trusts, foundations, and international business corporations), as we discussed earlier. As your businesses grow and you utilize these complex business structures, you will be in the winner's circle. Your assets will be protected from frivolous lawsuits and other predators.

Diversification for Safety

Once or twice a year, I used to attend international conferences where wealthy people do their continuing education. Wealthy people learn from other wealthy people, and now middle-class people are beginning to participate in these wealth symposiums and glean from them.

One speaker delivered an excellent presentation on diversification for safety. In our previous section, we talked about these stair steps to wealth: insurance and assurance, emergency funds, and capital guaranteed investments. When you become wealthy, you can invest in the speculative investments that are high yield but also high risk. This gentleman gave us the chart that you see below:

Silver & gold—30%

Cash—10%

Low yield investments—25%

Profitable real estate—25% (maybe in other countries)

High risk/high yield investments—10% (oil, water, agriculture)

He became wealthy by diversifying his assets in the manner shown above. If you notice, he has very little in cash, because the (Federal Reserve manipulated) "US" dollar is steadily losing its value all over the world. In a global economy, we need to think about wealth from a global perspective and make sure we have access to silver, gold, and other currencies. Low yield investments and real estate were his next most important investments, and the high yield investments were last; tied with cash. This formula worked for him and many others, and it can work for you as you become disciplined and start to implement the strategy.

High Yield Investments

There are many high yield investments out there that do pay off. Just because the middle-class is not told about them, or just because they always hear about the investments that go belly up does not mean that the high yield market is not making other people millions of dollars each year. Some of these investments earn 100% per year; however, I hope that you follow the strategies mentioned earlier and walk, don't run when your goal is to invest. If you take it slow and safe, the safe investments will pay off and you will eventually have extra money to try some of the high yield/high risk investments.

So, what specifics can I give you on asset protection and investing?

I wish I could, but because I am not licensed I can't go into detail about the wonderful investment opportunities that I have been privy to examine. If you contact me after you complete this book, I will be happy to share information with you about places to explore asset protection, investing, and international real estate.

SO, HOW DO THE WEALTHY STAY WEALTHY?

- They invest in gold, silver, and other precious metals.
- They invest in foreign exchange markets.
- They buy prime real estate in profitable U.S. markets.

- They buy international real estate.
- They start international Internet businesses.
- They invest in emerging technology offshore.
- They broker goods and services worldwide.
- They invest in their health (eat well, alternative medicine).
- They take advantage of exclusive SEC investments.
- They invest in oil and gasoline, solar, and wind power.
- They invest in water wells and water desalination.
- They invest in agricultural land.
- They invest in businesses with high profit potential.

Conclusion

We've reached the end of the book, so in closing, I will reveal to you your recipe for financial freedom. Bur first I want to congratulate you as a church pastor, administrator, or leader in being interested enough to find out how we can obtain additional finances, grow finances, and create wealth to expand the Kingdom. I pray that you take this teaching and pass it on to other Christians so that we can indeed be the head and not the tail. I am available for further teaching and instruction. Just contact me via my website—SherryPeelJackson.com, and I will gladly find out how I can serve you. My assignment in life is to help the Body of Christ in the financial arena so that we will have the resources to go and preach the gospel to the ends of the Earth.

Now, here is your recipe for Financial Freedom.

YOUR RECIPE FOR FINANCIAL FREEDOM

- Eliminate **Debt**
- Reduce **Taxes**
- Reduce Major **Expenses** Like Your Mortgage
- Create Wealth through International and Domestic **Investments**
- Protect Your Assets through **Proper Structuring**
- Increase Your **Income** to Match Your Goals
- Sustain Your Commitment to **Personal Growth**

I created this book because I see the Christian community suffering along with everyone else. We have the answer and we can't proclaim Christ as the answer if we are drowning in the same debt as the unsaved.

In addition, I feel that it is not fair for the wealthy to keep the secrets to themselves and leave the scraps for the middle-class. Now the middle-class can access the same wealth strategies as the wealthy have been for ages. If you are disciplined, patient, and willing to learn and implement the strategies discussed in this book, you can be on your way up the off-ramp and out of the rat race!

TWO POSSIBLE FUTURES

Here are two scenarios for you to ponder.

The Future of the Average Church

Pastor James and Beverly Patterson were finally on their way to achieving their life goals. James was now a full-time pastor at the church he founded two years ago, having quit his day job six months ago. Their new home was beautiful; it costs them $460,000 but according to the world standards, was well worth it. The tithes and offerings from the church were enough to cover the church mortgage and other bills, and a hefty enough salary for James to be at the church daily and for Beverly to only work part-time on her corporate job. They were finally part of the "in crowd"—that segment of full-time ministry leaders that hosted and attended conferences all over the region.

Beverly's part-time salary would pay the BMW lease and James would pay the Mercedes Benz note and the $3,700 per month mortgage payment. They had to accept a higher interest rate because they did not have perfect credit.

After 18 months in the house, there was a scandal at the church. One of the volunteer Sunday school teachers was accused of molesting a young girl, and instead of coming straight to the pastor about it, the young lady posted her experience on social media. The Sunday school teacher vehemently denied the allegations and said that the young lady was trying to get back at him because he embarrassed her during a Bible challenge tournament when she got a simple question wrong and the class laughed at her.

James and Beverly were caught off guard. They had only the minimum amount of church insurance in place, they didn't have a lawyer on call and they didn't have personal asset protection.

Not only was there a church split between those that believed the Sunday school teacher and those that believed the teenager, there was also a lawsuit filed against the church and the pastor by the girl's parents. The lawsuit claimed that it was the pastor's responsibility to protect the people in the flock, especially the young ones, while they were in the building.

The news of the allegations hit the local television and newspapers and half of the congregation left because Pastor Patterson refused to take sides. Within three-weeks the incident was over because the girl admitted to lying about the molestation. Her parents disciplined her, and they were forced to pay a fine for causing such a disruption. However, because of the sharp decrease in funds from people leaving the church Pastor James was no longer able to be a full-time pastor and keep the church alive at the same time. Brokenhearted and embarrassed he went back to his old job and they gladly accepted him back, only now at a salary that was over $10,000 less than his previous salary. Beverly was allowed to start working full time again, but the couple was not able to keep the house because they had gotten more than three months behind on the mortgage due to having to use all available funds to keep the church doors open.

The couple turned in the leased BMW and, although they took a hit on breaking the lease agreement, the $4,500 Buick Regal that they purchased took almost $600 off their monthly payments. The Mercedes Benz was sold to another pastor and the funds were used to pay off the funds owed to the dealership and get a small used Toyota Camry for James. They found a lovely two-bedroom rental home for $900 per month and they began to start over with the lessons learned about church and finances.

How many pastors and church leaders do you know who are just like this couple? How many of them will be able to overcome that situation without permanent damage to the church and to them personally?

In my travels and dealings with pastors, churches, and church leaders, this scenario is not unusual. Pastors and church leaders are in debt up to their ears with little or nothing in savings. The almighty VISA is used for any unplanned situations, with little thought of the future. When the church debt load is high the church may not survive serious financial challenges and could have to shut its doors.

No economy or individual can absorb forever the amount of debt that our economy is experiencing. The United States is deeper in debt than ever, yet we continue to go on as if everything is A-OKAY. The government's multi-trillion-dollar debt is set, unless Congress takes drastic measures (not happening). The congressmen making the decisions are wealthy for life; they have six-figure salaries, hefty retirement packages, and health care plans that are very different from the ones the government mandates for the rest of us. These congress people have trusts and foundations that are often "blind" to the public eye.

It's the church, along with the general public that's in trouble, swept away by the falling dollar, the volatile stock market, the student loan debt bubble, and the roller-coaster housing market. As people lose their jobs and are unable to pay their bills, the foreclosure rate has doubled. Those with money are buying property because they can pay cash, and as they do, former homeowners are forced to rent them. A little-known fact is that many foreigners, mostly Chinese, are buying up U.S. real estate like it's going out of style. Research the implications of that trend if you will.

Those who lose homes are flocking to apartments. The suicide and homicide rates are drastically increasing. If you don't believe this, look at what happened in Argentina in the early 1970s and what's happening in Venezuela and other countries now. The debt has outpaced the gross national product and they choose to print more money to pay the debt. Eventually their currency is worth less than the paper on which it was printed. Zimbabwe actually printed *ten million-dollar bills* when the economy collapsed in 2008. In the U.S., it is now against the law for people to melt down pennies and nickels. People found out that pennies and nickels were worth more melted down than in their coined state, and people were actually melting and selling them! To be sure, the economic meltdown has already started! (Update: Originally US pennies were 95% copper. Today US pennies are 97.5% cheap zinc and only

2.5% copper. Modern zinc pennies are toxic to dogs, parrots, and children, and are a symptom of the moral/financial health of the US government and the apathy of the US population.)

The point of this story is for you to figure out if this depicts you and your church, and to make you understand that you can and must do something about it. Time is of the essence.

The Future of the Financially Sound Church

You have this book to learn how to avoid the situation I just described, which is a classic tale of a church that did not prepare for the (uncertain) future.

Now you've learned how to become part of the many churches that are financially sound. What's going to happen when there is trouble in the church due to internal strife or interference from governmental agencies; when the economy dips to a critically low point and your members don't have the funds to give what's needed to maintain the normal functions of the church? If you've taken advantage of the strategies that you've learned in this book, you will be able to step over the obstacles and move forward with your family and your church intact.

You will understand the true definition of assets, and you will be able to buy James and Beverly's $460,000 home for $130,000, rent it out for monthly income, or hold it until prices rise and make a huge profit. Or, you will be able to buy a rental home in Costa Rica and stay there until the U.S. economy gets back on its feet!

If you use the knowledge that you learned in this book, you will be able to help your church members become financially free and they will teach their children and grandchildren. The Body of Christ will no longer lack the resources needed to spread the gospel to all the nations, and we will once again be the group that people turn to for answers to the questions of life.

If the home you live in is paid off, you can help your children and your grandchildren with college or business start-up expenses and with setting up their homes and their financial fortresses. This is what the wealthy do. I talk to the children of wealthy parents regularly. These young adults have been given the world on a silver platter, meaning the doors to opportunity are many and they are open. If the church is instrumental in teaching the principles of obtaining and maintaining wealth not only will the churches have more money to operate but there will be a proliferation of Christian businesses starting up, showing the world what business should be like—morally and ethically. Corruption would take a back seat to sound business principals. This is the vision that I see.

Christians will now be able to teach others how to take advantage of wealth building and asset protection strategies, have fun with it, and earn while enjoying it.

I do not intend to scare anyone with this book; I only want to let you know the severity of the problems we have in the United States. The economy will fail—sooner or later—but it will fail. What position will you hold? What shape will your church be in? Will it be the position of the average church, or of the financially sound church?

It's time for the church to rise up and take our place by force. It's time for Kingdom Advancement! Let's get started!!!

Now, let's explore a very informative chapter by my tax attorney, Nathan MacPherson!

UNDERSTANDING "SEPARATION OF CHURCH AND STATE": WHAT MUST A CHURCH RENDER UNTO CAESAR? NATHAN MCPHERSON, ATTORNEY AT LAW

My first exposure to the question of church taxation came at a very early age: I was baptized into Christ by my father's client who was the pastor of a local church. The IRS must not have liked his preaching, because it demanded he turn over the church's books and records, including the names and contact information of all of the members. The pastor rightly refused to turn over the membership list and my father litigated the issue and won on First Amendment grounds.

In the same year that my baptizing pastor rested in the Lord, my father took our family to Manhattan for the criminal trial of Larry Ranucci, Bishop of the Life Science Church of New York.[1] I was five years old at the time and remember eating my first pizza bagel in a New York diner,

1For more details about this case, see Chapter 12, New York Carpet Layer, of my father's book *Tax Fraud and Evasion: The War Stories,* available via www.BEAT-IRS.com learning about the Short Arms Disease,[2] and quietly sitting in the back of the courtroom while the prosecutors presented evidence regarding the unlawful nature of Larry's "Mail Order Ministry" business. You see, Larry was an Italian carpet layer who created a multilevel marketing business selling allegedly tax-exempt "churches" through the mail to lay people such as New York City police officers, garbage collectors, and bus drivers. By the time the case went to trial, over $8 million in revenue had flowed through the Life Science Church of New York, which was in reality no church at all. After a two-and-one-half month trial and then jury deliberation lasting a few days, Larry was found guilty and sentenced to seven years in federal prison for conspiracy to evade income taxes and income tax evasion.[3]

Fast forward three decades, and I now represent pastors under IRS attack for organizing as a "corporation sole," pastors and elders who want to know whether their churches are required to file income tax returns, and pastors and their congregants seeking advice regarding their religious objection to obtaining social security numbers for their children. Common to all of these questions is the overarching question underlying church-state relations: jurisdiction.

I. CHURCH-STATE RELATIONS

The Declaration of Independence states it is a self-evident truth that, "all me . . . . are endowed by their Creator with certain inalienable rights." In other words, our rights come from God Almighty, maker of heaven and earth.[4] Such was the general consensus at least as late as 1892 when the Supreme Court held that "this is a Christian nation."[5] It is also clear that we are not, like the Old Testament Nation of Israel, a theocracy or theocratic monarchy. What, then, is the relationship between our federal government and the Church?

Is there really "a wall of separation between church and state"?

Recognizing that God is the source of all authority, and that He delegates certain authority based upon the relationships of the parties,[6] we can begin to address the seminal question: what authority does the federal government have over a church? This issue is addressed in what are called the "Establishment Clause" and the "Free Exercise Clause" of the First Amendment to the U.S. Constitution: "Congress shall make no law respecting an establishment of religion, or prohibiting the free exercise thereof."

Today, people often refer to a "wall of separation between church and state." While this makes for good sound bites, it does little to bring clarity to the question of church-state relations. What exactly is the nature of this wall? How high is it? Does this mean that Christians may not hold office, or that if they do, they have to disregard their faith when making decisions?[7]

The phrase stems from Thomas Jefferson's January 1, 1802, letter to the Danbury (Connecticut) Baptist Association, answering their October 7, 1801, inquiry as to his view, as newly elected President of the United States, on religious freedom. Jefferson's letter was quoted by the Supreme Court in *Reynolds v. United States,* 98 U.S. 145, 164 (1878) and again in *Everson v. Board of Education,* 330 U.S. 1, 16 (1947), two seminal First Amendment cases.

Let's look at the historical context of the inquiry by the Danbury Baptist Association and President Jefferson's response. As the Supreme Court explained, "Before the adoption of the Constitution, attempts were made in some of the colonies and States to legislate not only in respect to the establishment of religion, but in respect to its doctrines and precepts as well."[8] In fact, eight of the 13 colonies had state-sponsored religious denominations (five were Anglican/Episcopalian and three Puritan/Congregationalist) and the Colonial Governor of Virginia even established the Church of England as the official church of Virginia Colony and made it a crime to fail to attend church on Sunday.[9] Recall that the Pilgrims had fled to America because of religious persecution from Anglicans who disagreed with their Puritan faith and had enacted laws establishing the Church of England as the state church (establishment) and criminalizing the practice of the Puritan faith (free exercise). It was all repeated in the colonies! When, in 1784, the Virginia House of Delegates proposed legislation to raise taxes for the provision of Christian teachers, vocal opposition arose. "Mr. [James] Madison prepared a 'Memorial and Remonstrance,' which was widely circulated and signed, and in which he demonstrated 'that religion, or the duty we owe the Creator,' was not within the cognizance of civil government."[10] "At the next session, the proposed bill was not only defeated, but another, 'for establishing religious freedom,' drafted by Mr. [Thomas] Jefferson, was passed."[11] This, then, was the backdrop of the adoption of the First Amendment to the U.S. Constitution: *the notion that civil government has no authority over matters of conscience, but only over physical acts that harm others.* President Jefferson wrote in his wall of separation letter, "that the legislative powers of the government reach actions only, and not opinions." Or, as the Supreme Court put it, "Laws are made for the government of actions, and while they cannot interfere with mere religious belief and opinions, they may with practices."[12]

The proposition that civil government does have jurisdiction over *actions* but does not have jurisdiction over *matters of conscience* was not new. Martin Luther professed the same in his 1523 treatise *Secular Authority: To What Extent It Should Be Obeyed.*

> God has ordained the two governments: the spiritual, which by the Holy Spirit under Christ makes Christians and pious people; and the secular, which restrains the unchristian and wicked so that they are obliged to keep the peace outwardly . . . . The laws of worldly government extend no farther than to life and property and what is external upon earth. For over the soul God can and will let no one rule but himself. Therefore, where temporal power presumes to prescribe laws for the soul, it encroaches upon God's government and only misleads and destroys souls. We desire to make this so clear that everyone shall grasp it, and that the princes and bishops may see what fools they are when they seek to coerce the people with their laws and commandments into believing one thing or another.[13]

Neither did Luther invent this doctrine; he was echoing at least 1,100 years of Christian teaching, *e.g.,* the words of St. Augustine of Hippo:

> It is evident, then, that the oldness of the letter, in the absence of the newness of the spirit, instead of freeing us from sin, rather

> makes us guilty by the knowledge of sin. Whence it is written in another part of Scripture, "He that increases knowledge, increases sorrow," Ecclesiastes 1:18—not that the law is itself evil, but because the commandment has its good in the demonstration of the letter, not in the assistance of the spirit; and if this commandment is kept from the fear of punishment and not from the love of righteousness, it is servilely kept, not freely, and therefore it is not kept at all. For no fruit is good which does not grow from the root of love. If, however, that faith be present which works by love, Galatians 5:6 then one begins to delight in the law of God after the inward man, Romans 7:22 and this delight is the gift of the spirit, not of the letter; even though there is another law in our members still warring against the law of the mind, until the old state is changed, and passes into that newness which increases from day to day in the inward man, while the grace of God is liberating us from the body of this death through Jesus Christ our Lord.[14]

St. Augustine was merely echoing, and quoting from, the Scriptures, *e.g.,* Romans 10:17, "Then faith is by hearing, and hearing by the Word of Christ."

In sum: it is established law that civil government has no authority over matters of conscience but does have authority over physical actions in the civil realm. How does this play out in modern America, especially with regard to churches? We must start with the confidence that, "God hath not given to us the Spirit of fear, but of power, and of love, and of a sound mind."[15]

II. SHOULD A CHURCH INCORPORATE?

The Church is the body of Christ and each Christian a member thereof.[16] Thus, we live in the civil realm in two ways: as individuals and as a collective. As individuals, each of us is subject to the governing authorities and has a duty to obey the civil law as long as that law does not contradict clear teachings of Scripture.[17] The Church as a whole is manifest as bodies of believers who come together, whether as local parishes, synods, denominations, or otherwise. One or more people is given, from the collective, the authority to act on behalf of the collective when dealing with those outside of the collective. How should these collectives organize vis-à-vis the civil government?

In Publication 1828, "Tax Guide for Churches and Religious Organizations," the IRS clearly states that there is an *automatic exemption for churches:* "Churches . . . . are automatically considered tax exempt and are not required to apply for and obtain recognition of tax-exempt status from the IRS."[18] This statement in Pub. 1828 is a paraphrase of *§ 508(c)(1)(A)* of the Internal Revenue Code, which explicitly states that "churches, their integrated auxiliaries, and conventions or associations of churches" are exempt from applying for *501(c)(3)* status.[19] **In other words, the federal government says that churches do not need to apply for nonprofit status to be tax exempt.**

This begs two questions: what does IRS consider a church and what does it mean to be tax exempt?

What is a Church?

While various historic confessions of faith offer a definition of "church,"[20] IRS admits that the Code does not define the term.[21] However, IRS and court cases have come up with a 14-part test of factors to determine whether a body of people constitutes a "church" within the meaning of the Code and is thus, by operation of law, a tax-exempt body. As a simplification, if the general public thinks you are a church, you probably are. What we have historically thought of as a church, a local congregation of believers who hold regular Sunday services in which they sing hymns, read and preach from the Bible, and administer the Sacraments, is a church within the meaning of the code. The 14 attributes considered by IRS are as follows:[22]

- Distinct legal existence
- Recognized creed and form of worship
- Definite and distinct ecclesiastical government
- Formal code of doctrine and discipline
- Distinct religious history
- Membership not associated with any other church or denomination
- Organization of ordained ministers
- Ordained ministers selected after completing prescribed courses of study
- Literature of its own
- Established places of worship
- Regular congregations
- Regular religious services

- Sunday schools for the religious instruction of the young
- Schools for the preparation of its members

It should be noted that a body need not possess all of these attributes to be considered a church and thus automatically tax-exempt. However, the more attributes a body possesses, the more certainty there is that it holds an automatic tax-exempt status. Most actual "bricks-and-mortar" churches, whether they be Lutheran or Methodist, Baptist or Pentecostal, meet these requirements without question. When IRS hinted that it was challenging whether one of my clients, a Pentecostal Church, was a church within the meaning of the Code, I incorporated pretty much the entire doctrinal statement of the church into our Tax Court petition. This was both an opportunity to spread the Gospel and to prove our case; in my next conversation with IRS Counsel, he made it clear that there was no question that my client was a church within the meaning of the Code.

Should a Church Incorporate Under *§ 508(c)(1)(A)?*

What about *§ 501(c)(3)?*

I have heard of some organizations advertising services to incorporate churches under *26 U.S.C. 508(c)(1)(A).* This makes no sense; as stated above, that code section is the one that states that churches qualify automatically, by operation of law, as tax exempt under *§ 501(c)(3).* There is no such thing as incorporating under *§ 508;* it is an oxymoron.

Likewise, many tax experts advise incorporating under *§ 501(c)(3)* despite the fact that *§ 508* renders such incorporation unnecessary and, in fact, redundant. These experts often claim that such incorporation brings certainty: a letter from IRS stating that the particular corporation (church) is, in fact, tax exempt. However, when a church volunteers to be subject to *§ 501(c)(3),* that church must thereafter comply with all of the technicalities of the statute and its corresponding regulations. Think about it: if you voluntarily reject the automatic exemption of *§ 508,* then you do not get the benefit of automatic exemption! You now must keep and file paperwork with the IRS. Thus, choosing *§ 501(c)(3)* brings with it the uncertainty of complying with technicalities or risking loss of tax-exempt status. In my experience with pastors and elders, the burdens of compliance outweigh the benefits of the piece of paper. Indeed, by the time pastors and elders are consulting with me, it is because they have failed to comply with the legal requirements of official *§ 501(c)(3)* status.

Compliance Requirements

Sherry has done an excellent job setting forth the compliance requirements for churches, especially pointing out the need to keep the pastors' (and elders') personal income and assets separate from church income and assets. While non-incorporation relieves pastors and elders from some of the technical compliance requirements, it should be noted that churches are still required to issue Forms W-2 and 1099 the same as any other person or legal entity, and, as just reiterated, must maintain their books and records separate from those of any other person (whether human being or legal person such as a corporation).

Fiduciary Duty

It is obvious from Scripture the duty pastors and elders owe to the church body. Similarly, the law imposes a duty of exercising care—the Prudent Man Rule. No one may convert church property to his own personal use (see the 14-part test IRS uses to define "church") and conversely, the pastor and elders have a duty to preserve and protect church property. For instance, they have a duty to maintain the premises against the weather (by, say, repairing roof leaks and maintaining insurance policies) and to invest church funds wisely (e.g., not to bet the church building in a poker game and not to invest all of the church savings in cryptocurrency). Failure to exercise business prudence can expose them to personal liability.

One aspect of fiduciary duty is to be aware of bogus donation scams. I have had clients who have allegedly received donations from generous philanthropists, who merely requested in return that the charity (my clients) sign off on the donation by providing a donation receipt and signed IRS Form 8283 "Noncash Charitable Contributions." The problem is, the charity received nothing of substantive value, while the donor received a six-figure tax benefit. The charity's directors then had a duty to either correct their tax filings or, if possible, recover the claimed value of the donation.

Another aspect of fiduciary duty is to beware of securities laws when raising funds for religious purposes. In 2018, the Lutheran Church-Canada was accused by the Alberta Securities Commission of misleading investors. The Alberta-British Columbia District had formed an extension fund to raise money for construction of churches and schools by soliciting investments from members and others and investing nearly 75% of it in a church/school/senior living project east of Calgary. In 2015, that project sought bankruptcy protection, causing loss to the investors (many of them members of the local parishes). Query: is this really a church or a business?

Beware of UBIT

An old problem that is becoming more prevalent is that of Unrelated Business Income Tax (UBIT). Modern churches often have attached coffee bars, bookstores, and other income sources besides the traditional offering plate. In addition, it is common for churches to operate camps, retreat centers, and the like. When the income from these other sources becomes material, liability can arise in two ways: UBIT and loss of nonprofit status.

If unrelated business income exceeds $1,000 for the year, the church must file a Form 990-T. The church must pay estimated taxes if the UBIT is expected to be $500 or more for the year. Moreover, if the UBIT is so large that it begins to overshadow the donations, the church risks losing nonprofit status. At this point, the church starts to look more like the "Church of the Immaculate Deduction" than an actual church. This term comes from a Tax Court opinion quoting attorney William Cohan, who is like an uncle to me:

> "During direct examination of petitioner, his counsel asked him whether he ever considered calling his church the 'Church

> of the Immaculate Deduction.' Normally we would ignore imprudent sarcasm by a party's counsel. In this instance, however, the remark is too apt an embodiment of the cynicism expressed by petitioner toward the tax system and toward religion. No amount of testimony about petitioner's religious studies or his good deeds can overcome the inferences to be drawn from his submission of frivolous tax protest Forms 1040, the inconsistent statements as to whether his real and personal property was owned by him or by the church, and the total lack of plausibility of his claims that his income and his living expenses were attributable to the church."[23]

Consider: if donations from the offering plate are $52,000 per year but revenues from the bookstore, coffee shop, and snack bar are $520,000 per year, is this truly a church, or is it a business with a church attached to it? This is not to say that high UBIT automatically disqualifies a church. Rather, the higher the ratio of non-religious to religious income, the more suspect it looks, and thus the more punctilious and transparent the pastor and staff must be with their bookkeeping. Also, not all side income counts toward the UBIT. Income from a side business is not subject to the tax if any of the following three conditions is met:

1. nearly all of the work is performed by volunteers (non-paid workers);

2. the activity is largely done for the convenience of the congregation (example: a cafeteria inside a hospital or museum was probably put there for the convenience of the hospital or museum staff); or
3. the vast majority of items being sold were donated.[24]

Related to this is the "Public Support Test," stemming from *26 U.S.C. § 509.* Under this law, an organization does not qualify as a "private foundation" if it does not receive "public support"; that is, if too much of its income comes from one (or a few) sources rather than from the general public. If a church is actually a "church" supported by tithes from congregants, this will not be an issue.

Beware of the Vow of Poverty

We have represented several clients who took a "vow of poverty" not recognized by the IRS. Such cases can be brought by IRS as either criminal or civil; recall the criminal tax case of Larry Ranucci, Bishop of the Life Science Church of New York. Ranucci and his codefendant "ministers" paid no income taxes on over $3.5 million of income due to what the courts held to be sham vows of poverty and were sentenced to federal prison for tax evasion. Other clients have come under civil attack by IRS claiming back taxes, interest, and penalties (the interest and penalties can easily double and in some cases nearly triple the overall liability – the *§ 6663* fraud penalty alone is 75% of the tax).

The IRS recognizes as legitimate a vow of poverty if the following conditions are met: (a) the pastor must be working as an agent of his religious order, rather than for himself; (b) the pastor must remit the money to the religious order; and (c) the pastor must be engaged in work common for that religious order.[25]

In other words, when the pastor receives money from third parties he must do so as agent of the church and not in his individual capacity, the pastor must pay that money over to the church (with the church paying the pastor's living expenses), and the work undertaken by the pastor must be typical for the church. Think of monks in a monastery.

The courts have been clear that a pastor who works for a church (preaching on Sunday, holding Bible studies, etc.) and receives a salary for doing so does not qualify for tax exemption under the vow of poverty, even if he makes, and the church board accepts from him, a written vow of poverty. Much less does the owner of an automobile transmission repair shop, who names his shop "The Church of Transmission," qualify, even if he makes a written vow of poverty to "The Church of Transmission."[26]

Beware of the Corporation Sole

Many clients come to me because they have become entangled with the "corporation sole." There exists much confusion over this entity, and clients have told me, "But Washington law allows for the corporation sole!" Yes, this is true, the "corporation sole," just like the "corporation aggregate," is a legitimate legal entity. The text on the IRS Web page describing Revenue Ruling 2004-27 succinctly sums up the law on this matter:

> This ruling emphasizes to taxpayers, tax scheme promoters and return preparers that, while a "corporation sole" is a legitimate corporate form that may be used by a religious leader to hold property and conduct business for the benefit of the religious entity, a taxpayer cannot avoid income tax by establishing a religious organization for tax avoidance purposes.

Simply put, a corporation sole is a corporation with only one shareholder/director/officer. It is akin to the modern single-member Limited Liability Company and can be contrasted with the traditional corporation that has multiple shareholders who elect a board of directors who appoint officers to run the corporation.

While it is certainly lawful for a local parish to organize as a corporation sole, doing so does not magically render the pastor's (or other incorporator's) income and assets tax exempt. Indeed, in 2004 the IRS issued a consumer alert warning people about scams promoting the unlawful use of the "Corporation Sole" laws. To restate from above: the church must maintain an existence separate and distinct from its pastor, deacons, members, etc.; the church's nonprofit status does not apply to the pastor, deacons, or anyone else. Moreover, because a corporation sole is an entity created under state law, it may not be the best choice for a church; historically, churches have organized as common law trusts. Those wishing to form a new parish should consult competent legal advice on the best way to organize their parish.

III. FREE SPEECH

While Sherry addressed the question of political speech, it is important and worth discussing again here. 26 *U.S.C. § 501(c)(3)* specifically excludes from the definition of exempt organization any group that does, "participate in, or intervene in (including the publishing or distributing of statements), any political campaign on behalf of (or in opposition to) any candidate for public office." IRS Publication 1828 clarifies the position of IRS on this as relates to issues of public policy:

> "The political campaign activity prohibition isn't intended to restrict free expression on political matters by leaders of churches or religious organizations speaking for themselves, as individuals. Nor are leaders prohibited from speaking about important issues of public policy."[27]

It is incumbent upon pastors to preach the full counsel of God's Word,[28] specifically to sound the alarm as to those issues particularly affecting his congregation.[29] Ezekiel 33:3–6 provides sobering words regarding the duty to speak God's Word: if the watchman fails to sound the alarm, the blood is on his hands; if he sounds the alarm but the people fail to listen, the blood is on their hands.

Many of the issues that have in recent decades created doubt in the promises God makes in His Word have also become political issues. Just as the serpent, the Old Evil Foe, said to Eve, "Did God really say . . . ?"[30], so today, society and politicians ask us, "Did God really say . . . thou shalt have no other gods before Me? . . . thou shalt not murder the preborn . . . . marriage is only between one man and one woman?" This begs the question: may a pastor lawfully preach on these issues without risking loss of his church's nonprofit status?

First of all, we must stand on the firm foundation of God's Word. Jesus' parting Words to His Church were to make disciples of all nations by baptizing them and teaching them to obey everything He commanded.[31] Thus, irrespective of what IRS says, pastors have a duty to obey Jesus first.[32] And keep in mind what we are talking about: *the price of a pastor's free reign at preaching the full scope of his calling and conscience is merely that his congregants' tithes might not be tax deductible on their individual income tax returns and that the church will be taxed on its profit, if any.* That's all. But his preaching likely is not a problem anyway, because the answer to this question hinges first upon what we discussed previously—whether the particular church is actually a church.

Recall the IRS' 14-part test of what it means to be a church. A pastor preaching Law and Gospel from the pulpit, proclaiming that God says "thou shalt not murder," and offering the repentant murderer forgiveness for the sin of murder through the shed blood of Jesus does not run afoul of Title 26. Conversely, a "church" whose sole purpose is to ensure the election of Candidate Bob who is running for Congress is going to have a hard time defending its nonprofit status.

In fact, both Title 26 and Publication 1828 address the issue of campaigning for a particular candidate, not advocating positions. Recall the fact that the government does not have jurisdiction over belief. Preaching on issues is not prohibited to nonprofits; electioneering for a particular candidate is. Additionally, the restriction against campaigning for a particular candidate is against the church itself—and thus the pastor or elders only when they are acting in their official capacity for the church—and not against the individuals personally. Thus, a pastor may write an op-ed article in the local paper, or attend political rallies, or donate to a candidate in his personal capacity. He merely may not use church funds or a church publication to do so, and if/when he does write an op-ed, etc., he should indicate that he is not acting in his official capacity; *i.e.,* that he is speaking for himself personally and not on behalf of the church.

IV. CONCLUSION

The bottom line for pastors and other church leaders is summed up in the 17th-century hymn by Johann Heinrich Schröder, "One thing's needful,"[33] quoting from Jesus' Words to Martha in Luke 10:42a, "But one thing is needful." If a church truly is devoted to preaching Christ crucified,[34] it will qualify as a nonprofit as a matter of law and will not be engaged in taxable activities as a matter of practice. The problems arise when church leadership remove their eyes from Jesus and become distracted by earthly matters.[35]

While it should go without saying, the voluminous civil and criminal case law demonstrates that it does not: the Church is not a means to shield income from taxation. Pastors, deacons, and others must keep their personal finances separate from church finances and not use their church as a means to avoid personal taxation.

God has given to the Church the authority to preach His Word and God has given to civil government the authority to secure the right to life, liberty, and property. To the extent that the Church operates within the civil realm—such as by employing people—she must follow the civil law—such as issuing Forms W-2 and 1099. However, as long as a parish or other church body operates as a real church, it, and donations made to it, qualify under 26 *U.S.C. § 501.*

Endnotes

1 For more details about this case, see Chapter 12, New York Carpet Layer, of my father's book, *Tax Fraud and Evasion: The War Stories,* available via www.BEAT-IRS.com

2 Larry would tell us about an associate who would never pay for lunch, "He's got the Short Arms Disease. He's got the money in his pockets but his arms are too short!"

3 *U.S. v. Ebner,* 782 F.2d 1120, 1123 (2nd Cir. 1986) (affirming the convictions of Bishop Larry Ranucci and his fellow "ministers.").

4 Jeremiah 32:17, Acts 17:24.

5 *Church of the Holy Trinity v. United States,* 143 U.S. 457, 471 (1892).

6 It is both a biblical and a Common Law principle that the relationship of the parties determines their rights and duties.

7 The answer to those two questions is a resounding, "No!" As Justice Rehnquist wrote, "There is simply no historical foundation for the proposition that the framers intended to build a wall of separation [between Church and State]. . . .The recent court decisions are in no way based on either the language or intent of the framers. . . . The "crucible of litigation". . . is well adapted to adjudicating factual disputes on the basis of testimony presented in court, but no amount of repetition of historical errors in judicial opinions can make the errors true. The "wall of separation between Church and State" is a metaphor based on bad history, a metaphor which has proved useless as a guide to judging. It should be frankly and explicitly abandoned." *Wallace v. Jaffree,* 472 U.S. 38, at 107, 105 S.Ct. 2479, at 2516 (1985), William Rehnquist, J., dissenting.

8 *Reynolds,* 98 U.S. at 162.

9 Laws enacted by the First General Assembly of Virginia in August of 1619. See H. R. McIlwaine and John P. Kennedy, eds.,

Journals of the House of Burgesses of Virginia, vol. 1 (Richmond, 1905), 9–14.

10 *Reynolds* at 163.

11 *Id.*

12 *Id.* at 166. Query what this means as to the "free exercise" of religion.

13 Martin Luther, *Secular Authority: To What Extent It Should Be Obeyed,* Part I, Sec. 4 (January 1, 1523).

14 St. Augustine of Hippo, *On the Spirit and the Letter,* Chapter 26 (A.D. 412).

15 2 Timothy 1:7.

16 "Now you are the body of Christ and individually members of it" (1 Corinthians 12:27).

17 See, *e.g.,* Romans 13 ("Let every soul be subject unto the higher powers: for there is no power but of God: and the powers that be, are ordained of God. . . ."); 1 Peter 2:13–14 ("Therefore submit yourselves unto all manner ordinance of man for the Lord's sake, whether it be unto the King, as unto the superior, Or unto governors, as unto them that are sent of him, for the punishment of evil doers, and for the praise of them that do well."); Acts 5:29
("Then Peter and the Apostles answered, and said, We ought rather to obey God than men.").

18 IRS Publication 1828, "Tax Guide for Churches and Religious Organizations," page 2.

19 "Mandatory Exceptions Subsections (a) and (b) [requiring application with the IRS for recognition of 501(c)(3) status] shall not apply to—(A) churches, their integrated auxiliary, and conventions or associations of churches."

20 They are in general agreement that the Church consists of all Christians. *See, e.g.,* Art. VII and VIII of the Augsburg Confession of 1530, "The Church is the congregation of saints, in which the Gospel is rightly taught and the Sacraments are rightly administered . . . [T]he Church properly is the congregation of saints and true believers. . . ."

21 IRS Publication 1828, "Tax Guide for Churches and Religious Organizations," page 1.

22 Taken from the IRS Website https://www.irs.gov/charities-non-profits/churches-religious-organizations/churches-defined.

23 *Duck v. Commissioner,* 47 T.C.M. 1654, 1657 (1984).

24 *26 CFR 1.513-1(e).*

25 *See* Rev. Rul. 77-290, 1977-2 C.B. 26 (1977) and Rev. Rul. 76-323, 1976-2 C.B. 18.

26 *U.S. v. Ebner,* 782 F.2d 1120, 1123 (2nd Cir. 1986) (affirming the convictions of Bishop Larry Ranucci and his fellow "ministers.")

27 IRS Publication 1828, page 8.

28 Acts 20:26–27, "Therefore I testify to you this day that I am innocent of the blood of all, for I did not shrink from declaring to you the whole counsel of God."

29 As Martin Luther stated, "If you preach the Gospel in all aspects with the exception of the issues which deal specifically with your time—you are not preaching the Gospel at all."

30 Genesis 3:1, "Now the serpent was more subtle than any beast of the field, which the Lord God had made: and he said to the woman, 'Yea, hath God indeed said, ye shall not eat of every tree of the garden?' "

31 Matthew 28:18–20, "And Jesus came, and spake unto them, saying, All power is given unto me, in heaven, and in earth. Go therefore, and teach all nations, baptizing them in the Name of the Father, and the Son, and the Holy Ghost, Teaching them to observe all things, whatsoever I have commanded you: and lo, I am with you alway, until the end of the world, Amen."

32 (Acts 4:19), "But Peter and John answered unto them, and said, Whether it be right in the sight of God, to obey you rather than God, judge ye."

33 "One thing's needful; Lord, this treasure, Teach me highly to regard . . . How were Mary's thoughts devoted, Her eternal joy to find, As intent each word she noted, At her Savior's feet reclined! How kindled her heart, how devout was its feeling, While hearing the lessons that Christ was revealing! All earthly concerns she forgot for her Lord, And found her contentment in hearing His Word."

34 I Corinthians 1:23a, "But we preach Christ crucified. . . .

35 See, e.g., Hebrews 12:2, "Looking unto Jesus the author and finisher of our faith, who for the joy that was set before him, endured the cross, and despised the shame, and is set at the right hand of the throne of God." See also Luke 10:38–42.

Christ was revealing! All earthly concerns she forgot for her Lord, And found her contentment in hearing His Word."

About the Author

Sherry Peel Jackson is a retired certified public accountant, certified fraud examiner, and former IRS agent with over 30 years of experience in public, private, and governmental accounting. She is a financial and business coach who conducts basic and advanced financial education seminars across the United States. She also instructs IRS audit information and preparation workshops for various establishments, including private companies, non-profit organizations, and churches. Ms. Jackson has over 20 years of experience with church accounting and policy, pastor's personal finances, and church wealth creation strategies. She has conducted church compliance audits, presented on various topics at several ministry workshops, and created strategic plans for churches in Metro Atlanta and beyond.

Ms. Jackson is a licensed minister with a Master of Arts in Christian Studies from Luther Rice University & Seminary in Lithonia, Georgia. She graduated Summa Cum Laude and was awarded the Dianne Mixon Scholarship for Women and received the Who's Who Among Students In American Universities & Colleges award. Ms. Jackson also earned an executive certificate from the Howard

University Executive Leadership for Ministers Program, where she increased her business knowledge in the areas of financial management, strategic planning, legal and ethical issues, and ministry analytics. She is a licensed Chaplain and is pursuing her Doctorate in Christian Education at Andersonville Theological Seminary in Camilla, Georgia.

Ms. Jackson is also a Christian author and speaker. She is the author of several books including: *How to Escape the Rat Race: Four Keys to Acquire the Life of Your Dreams, How to Stick It to the IRS: Confessions From a Former Insider, and Basic Financial Survival: Learning to Survive Then Thrive in Any Economy.*

Ms. Jackson has developed educational courses that will enlighten individuals and churches about proper techniques to go beyond surviving and begin thriving. In her coaching and workshops, she teaches entrepreneurship, debt-free living, audit and asset protection, and survival in the new economy. She lives in Stone Mountain, Georgia.

Made in United States
Orlando, FL
04 November 2026

90219746R00139